Hygge

A guide to happy living with recipes and tips

igloobooks

*Published in 2017
by Igloo Books Ltd
Cottage Farm
Sywell
NN6 0BJ
www.igloobooks.com*

Copyright © 2017 Igloo Books Ltd

*All rights reserved. No part of this publication may be
reproduced or transmitted in any form or by any means,
electronic, or mechanical, including photocopying, recording,
or by any information storage and retrieval system,
without permission in writing from the publisher.
The measurements used are approximate.*

*HUN001 0817
2 4 6 8 10 9 7 5 3 1
ISBN 978-1-78670-909-7*

*Designed by Charlie Wood-Penn
Edited by Richard Davis*

Printed and manufactured in China

Contents

	Introduction	4
Chapter 1	Say hello to hygge	6
Chapter 2	The hygge home	16
Chapter 3	Hygge food	38
Chapter 4	Hygge activities	74
Chapter 5	Hygge through the seasons	84
Chapter 6	Hygge Christmas	100
Chapter 7	Family and friends	110
Chapter 8	Follow that thought	118
	Index	128

Introduction

Much has been said about the Danes being some of the happiest people in the world. They have vied with their close neighbours, the Norwegians, for years, claiming the top spot on the World Happiness Report several times during the second decade of this century. Fellow Scandinavians and north Europeans, Sweden, Iceland, and Finland, all feature in the top ten. So what is it about these snowy nations, that spend their winters in darkness, that makes them so content? The answer might lie in their outlook on winter warmth and summer sun: hygge.

What is hygge?

Hygge is a warm and welcoming thing that makes life better in the simplest of ways. Hygge sounds a little like hug – and that's no coincidence: hygge is a way of taking the time to feel safe and happy, and to enjoy the warmth and security of being with people you love. There is great happiness to be found in having a snowball fight, reading a good book while the rain hammers on the windows, or playing charades with generations of family joining in. Specifically Danish, but intrinsically Scandinavian, hygge is something that the north Europeans embrace as part of their everyday living.

> We can all benefit from hygge, by learning to be "in the moment" and counting our blessings: not because we were given a promotion or a pay rise, or upgraded our car, or trained for a marathon, but for much smaller joys in life.

Chapter 1
Say hello to hygge!

Hygge is a concept that is understood throughout Scandinavia, but its fame is spreading around the globe. Norwegians, and especially Danes, use it a lot to describe how they are feeling, what they are doing, and what is going on around them.

Hygge history

The word "hygge" has its roots in Old Norse, when the Viking word *hyggja* meant "to think and be satisfied with". It is also linked to the Old English word *hycgan*, meaning "to think and to consider". The original Norwegian word meant "well-being", and might itself come from the word "hugge" meaning "to embrace". Hygge's modern sense is a mixture of all these things and more, encompassing cosiness, security, relaxing and enjoying the moment.

Say it out loud

So, how do we say it? To pronounce "hygge", start with a nice breathy "h" followed by an "oo" and a "g". Tag an "uh" on the end: hoo-guh. If you want to add authenticity, make sure the "oo" is pronounced with your lips fully pursed, as if you were saying the sound at the end of the word "view".

Simple pleasures

Hygge has been put in the spotlight recently (something which is completely against its nature) and lauded as a possible route to happiness. The essence of hygge is uncomplicated. It is about enjoying those situations when you feel settled and relaxed, where you stop worrying about the future, and focus on the important things: friends, family, and food… hygge is a lot about food. You will get a better sense of what hygge is all about as you read further.

It's a crazy world

Life in the twenty-first century is super fast! So many people work long hours, travel great distances, eat too much and too quickly, and spend less time with their friends and family than previous generations did. Hygge works as an antidote to all of that. It is refreshing to leave behind the stresses of the week and spend the weekend cocooned, both physically and emotionally. You don't need a log cabin, a lake or snow on the ground – despite the media images of hygge – your own home can be your safe place, whatever and wherever it is.

All together now

If you introduce hygge into your life, you are making a conscious decision to make time just for you and what is really important to you. Hygge is popular because it encourages people to slow down, kick back, and take a moment. A hygge way of life is about being together – properly together, with real people, not on social media – and enjoying each other's company. It's meeting up with friends that you'd like to see more of, and making your children and your partner put down their phones and talk to you. It's about laughing and playing, looking around you and really seeing what's there, and – even if it sounds scary – letting down your guard.

All by myself

Having said that, you can absolutely enjoy "hyggelig" moments when no one else is around. There are times when you simply step off the treadmill and stop for a while, taking in your surroundings and searching for an inner calm. Different people do this in different ways, for what is "hyggelig" to one person may not work for another. Reading, knitting, cooking, baking, doing a crossword, writing a letter, walking the dog, pottering in the garden: are they chores or opportunities to unwind and chill out? They can be either, they can be both – it all depends on your frame of mind at that moment.

Hygge harmony

One important thing to remember is that hygge is not a competition and certainly not a grind. Nobody needs to out-do another, whether it be by laying on a feast, talking too much or too loudly, or having the nicest home. The very essence of hygge is found in sharing: sharing the floor, sharing your memories, sharing the cooking, sharing the moment.

Spoil your senses

The sensory world is extremely important for hygge. Open up to the sights, smells, and sounds around you. Notice how things feel and taste. Comfort food is so-called because of the feeling it gives you, and the smell of bread in the oven, a Sunday roast, or a freshly baked cake cooling on the rack all increase the anticipation of how good they are going to be when you sit down to eat. Sitting down is vital – food just doesn't taste the same, or give as much satisfaction, if you eat on the move.

Open your ears

One of the greatest sounds is silence. As you curl up in your favourite hyggelig spot, close your eyes and listen. Blissful, peaceful, quiet. Then you can start to notice other sounds: children playing in the school down the street; rain pattering on the rooftops or pounding on the pavement; the crackle of an open fire; birds singing; even traffic in the distance – people going about their business while you have five minutes to yourself. That's a hygge mindset, right there in the middle of life's hustle and bustle.

A consumer contradiction

Much of what you read about hygge will be about creating the mood. It's true, you can build a hyggelig home filled with candles and cushions, woollen throws, and wood-burning

stoves. Really, though, hygge is tied to an emotion or an atmosphere: a feeling, an experience, a sense of "being". You don't need "stuff" to make it happen. Ironically, today's consumer-led world has seized on the concept of hygge to try to sell us more things, with hygge shops popping up here and there, but don't fall for it. Belongings don't bring hygge; people do.

Making memories

Consider those people for whom you find it hard to buy presents because they already have everything they need. They don't want more nick-nacks to clutter their home or more possessions to find space for. A much better gift is an experience that creates memories – an outing with the whole family or a trip to see something new. Putting time aside to be together, and planning a day's activities that everyone will enjoy, is a gift to people who really don't want anything in a material sense.

"If you want to feel rich, just count the things you have that money can't buy"

– Proverb

Hygge happiness

The concept of hygge is important in Denmark because of the long, dark winters and relatively short summers. When the cold is biting and daylight is limited, it is comforting to know that warmth and sparkle can be found in many ways. Denmark famously scores highly on the happiness chart, topped at times by its equally hygge neighbour, Norway. Despite their climate, or possibly because of it, the residents of Denmark and Norway value time spent on outdoor pursuits, followed by a cosy gathering in front of an open fire, with candles and card games. Luckily for other nations, the Danes and Norwegians have allowed us to borrow this feeling.

Complete hygge

Hygge is so much a part of the Danish national psyche that they use it all the time, as an action, a description, and in many delicious compound words: a "hyggekrog" is a favourite cosy corner, where you can sit for a "hyggestund" wearing your "hyggesokken" and "hyggebukser". A rough translation is: have a moment of happy downtime wearing your favourite woollen socks and comfy trousers.

Turn off technology

Sharing the hygge is a timely and welcome contrast to the chaos and tumult of modern life. It's difficult to be relaxed and happy when you are caught up in a cycle of work, gym, electronics, and then bed. TV dinners, microwave meals, fast food and endless appointments and deadlines are all the enemy of enjoyable family time. A 2013 survey found that only 40% of families eat together three times a week, and more than one in five families do so in front of the TV. A study in 2015 found that teenagers in the UK spend more than 27 hours a week online, almost three times longer than their counterparts a decade before. The rise in awareness of hygge suggests it's time to buck the trend, switch off, and settle down together to swap stories and share your thoughts.

Talk time

Nobody is saying that hygge happens all the time. It's hard when you have to feed a family of four at separate times to ensure they all get to athletics, ballet, and football on a Wednesday evening. Having said that, a ten-minute drive to the training ground is the perfect opportunity to catch up on your teenager's day. Your child will know he or she isn't captive for too long. Seize that moment and enjoy it!

A new outlook on life

Of course, being happy is good for you and those around you. Hygge isn't so much a way of life that can be adopted, but a way of looking at life to recognise the best bits. Enjoying the moment and knowing how to switch off can improve your mental health, and laughing is scientifically proven to reduce stress hormones, such as epinephrine and cortisol, and increase the release of mood-enhancing endorphins. Take a tip from the Danes and spend more time outdoors. If there were a top ten of hygge enhancers, fresh air and exercise would be in it.

Heading out

All the advocates of hygge enjoy the physical side of life. Cycling and walking are two of the mainstays of a Scandinavian existence. You can feel the benefits to your heart and muscles as you explore outdoors or travel to work using your own pedal power. Don't use the weather as an excuse to stay inside. The Danes certainly don't! They head to the countryside as often as they can, come snow or shine. Britain may not be renowned for its winter pursuits, but has many more clement days to take a stroll in the park, hire a boat on a river, or simply pack up a picnic and cycle until you find a patch of green to sit upon.

Modern hygge

If you're thinking that this all sounds a bit eco-friendly, then you're right. Taking less from our wonderful planet, whether it is fuel, water, clean air, or wild land, is a very hygge-friendly approach to modern life. If you can learn to love the old items in your home instead of coveting new ones, your surroundings will be filled with memories and familiar friends, like the battered leather sofa you have owned since your children were born. Reuse, repair, redistribute, repurpose, recycle – the key to satisfaction is in the "re" at the start of all those words.

Back to basics

Cooking hearty food for your loved ones is also a very hyggelig thing to do. It fits the new-from-old recommendation that we prepare more food from scratch, using seasonal ingredients, that we now acknowledge is better both for our bodies and our world. Shop around for food from sustainable sources and local growers, and spend an afternoon pottering with friends in the kitchen, using up any collective overstock of fresh fruit and vegetables before they go to waste.

Chapter 2
The hygge home

Your home should be a refuge and a place where you feel the most hyggelig. The aim is to create a place of warmth and tranquility where you can look after those to whom you are closest, as well as favourite friends whom you invite into your haven. When you close the doors and curtains, you shut out the rest of the world. This isn't because you don't care, but because sometimes you need to nurture yourself and your loved ones.

It's cold outside

In the depths of winter, a cosy home makes you feel more secure. Feeling warm gives a sense of safety, while feeling cold is linked to fear and vulnerability. There are different ways to warm your home. The classic hygge way is with an open fire or a wood-burning stove. As a heat source, an open fire is inefficient, which is why stoves are increasing in popularity. Stoves provide the same focal point for a room, and a mesmerising glow and crackle that tempt you to stop what you are doing and simply gaze at the flames.

Stack it up

Experiment with different types of wood. Yew, pine, apple, cherry, and birch all give off a wonderful scent as they burn. Stack your wood in a covered store that remains open at the sides to allow it to dry out evenly. Wood should be seasoned for at least a year before you throw it on the fire. Enjoy a rustic display of logs next to your fireplace – but ensure it is dry and clean before bringing it indoors to prevent the introduction of mould and decay.

Feel the heat

If real fires aren't for you and your home, don't be discouraged. Feeling the heat through your feet with underfloor heating systems, which bring an unexpected glow of pleasure, while central heating undoubtedly serves its purpose to heat your surroundings. Curling up with a book next to a radiator is still satisfying.

"Surely everyone is aware of the divine pleasures which attend a wintry fireside; candles at four o'clock, warm earth rugs, tea…whilst the wind and rain are raging audibly without"

- Thomas de Quincey

Fuel rules

Many UK homes are located in smoke-controlled areas, where only authorised fuels are allowed. You should check with your council before installing a stove or burning coal and wood. Once you are given the go-ahead, you can then enjoy the sensory experience of alluring smells, sputtering sounds, dancing flames and glowing embers that your stove will provide. A good fire appeals to your senses and your heart in equal measures.

> "That light we see is burning in my hall. How far that little candle throws his beams! So shines a good deed in a naughty world"
>
> - William Shakespeare, The Merchant of Venice

Lighting

Candles are the essence of hygge, and for good reason: light is at a premium through the dark winter months but it adds to the feeling of security as you return home from the world outside. Many Danish homes still keep lit candles by the door, both to welcome people as they enter and to act as a guide to passers-by. It is a simple thing to do for yourself: light a candle on a windowsill, or use LED tea lights or a string of ornamental bulbs in a jar.

A candlelit scene

The Danes light candles on winter mornings and summer nights, indoors and outdoors, in the workplace, and at home. More than a quarter of the Danish population light candles every day, and nearly a third of people light more than five candles at one time. The Danish tend towards natural and organic candles made of beeswax or vegetable wax rather than paraffin wax. The British are following in hot pursuit, but often prefer to burn coloured or scented candles. There is nothing wrong with this; if the smell of sandalwood or vanilla is hygge for you, then that's absolutely fine.

Candle care

It goes without saying that you need to take care with open flames. Keep them away from curtains and other cloth and, to avoid soot stains and fire hazards, don't burn them on a shelf with another shelf overhead. Ensure they are on a heatproof surface as the base could become hot or wax may drip down the sides. Don't burn candles for too long either – between two and four hours is long enough. Treat your candles well: trim the wick before you light it, to around a 0.5 centimetres long. This will increase the quality of the flame and reduce the soot that is given off.

Low-level lighting

Candles not only provide light, but they create a mood within a room. If you don't want to light candles, this can be achieved with low-wattage lamps and even well-placed LED light strips. Don't banish bright lights completely – they are needed in a workspace such as the kitchen, study, studio, or by the bathroom mirror – but have an alternative so you can create layers of light as needed. Overhead lighting can be harsh, so use lamps at different levels for a more comforting glow.

Hygge in your house

Some images of a hygge home are ones of busy rooms with much-loved items everywhere. Others portray a decluttered, minimalist space with a few well-chosen belongings on display. Each is equally valid; it depends what works for your sense of style versus comfort. There are, however, some tried-and-tested ways to decorate a room for the maximum sense of well-being.

Textiles and textures

When your colour scheme is neutral, it is important to introduce a variety of textures. Use traditional textiles with a touchy-feely quality to them: felt, worsted, tweed, velvet, tartan and corduroy. They have the added gravitas of history and a sense of resoluteness to contribute to the overall feeling of safety and protection. Mix it up with soft, textured curtains, a leather sofa and felt lampshades.

Adding throws

A basic room can be transformed into a cosy cave with the addition of soft furnishings such as rugs, cushions and throws. A rug pulls together the elements of a room, bringing disparate items closer in an intimate collaboration. Cushions and throws are the ultimate hyggelig soft furnishings, allowing you to curl up in comfort and warmth as you take time out. This is where you can really play with textures. A sheepskin rug is both primitive and seductive at the same time. There is a huge variety of tactile cushions available, from faux fur and bouclé to velour and shiny satin. Throws and blankets in chenille, brushed cotton, mohair, teddy bear fleece, cashmere or chunky cable knits can be draped across the back of a chair, ready to snuggle into on cold nights or wintery days. Stick to neutral shades with a flash of colour in the check or weave.

Colours of comfort

The essence of hygge is feeling relaxed and at one with nature or your surroundings. For that reason, calming, earthy, neutral colours such as grey, cream, white and beige are popular. Warm them up with accents from nature. Green and brown are fresh and bright. Flower colours – pink, red, purple, orange, and peach – add a rosy glow. Shades of blue and turquoise are soothing and calming, while yellows are the colour of sunshine. To keep the room light and airy, rather than dark and overbearing, play with the paler versions of the colour palette.

Cosy corners

Find your favourite place and make it your "hygge zone". It may well be somewhere small and contained, such as a bay window, a nook or alcove, a corner of a larger room, or just a favourite chair in front of the fire. Open-plan living might not seem to lend itself to this, but clever positioning of furniture can provide a small place of sanctuary; use curtains, shelves and screens as dividers if necessary. Find the sun and establish your cosy corner where the warmth is. As a general rule of thumb, follow your pets: dogs and especially cats are particularly good at finding the sunniest, most snug place in the house.

Kitting it out

You can make your cosy corner work for you by adding personal touches. Books, cushions, candles, photos, and blankets can all help you find peace and tranquility after a busy day. Bring nature indoors with flowers and greenery as well as with items you have collected on your adventures: stones, shells, pinecones, driftwood and twigs. Wood is in itself a comforting substance, so make the most of wooden floors, doors, window frames and furniture. UPVC is not so hygge, so drape modern window seats with curtains and bunting if necessary.

Furniture choices

Stark, modernist seating is unlikely to entice you to kick off your shoes and curl into a ball. Make the most of much-loved pieces, whether passed down through the family, or that have simply been in your home for years. Look for furniture that wraps itself around you or allows you to sink deep into its embrace. High-backed chairs were once designed to keep away draughts, but these days they offer solitude and privacy. Don't reject modern versions: retro pod chairs, Chesterfield-inspired wingback chairs, sofas influenced by the historical Knole settee and the Danish classic Arne Jacobsen egg chair all look stunning and feel even better to sit in.

> Many of my hygge moments have been spent curled up on my bed in the mid-afternoon sun. The warmth on my skin, the view from my window, the buzz of the world going about its business outside – they all contribute to a wonderful glow of contentment that lifts my spirits. I haven't made any changes to my room, although it is decorated in soothing shades of grey and white – but it has unconsciously become my go-to place to wind down and reflect on the good things of the day.

Viva vintage!

Old furniture can be like a familiar friend after a long day on your feet. Keepsakes and mementoes are comforting, reminding you of good friends and good times. As you take stock of your surroundings and make the necessary switches for your new hygge mindset, remember that your home has evolved and grown with you over the years. Don't throw that all away by reinventing your décor. If your house is very modern, cheat a little by adding carefully chosen vintage items. Old suitcases are great for storage; vintage china adds charm to your coffee and cake get-togethers with friends; an old-fashioned rocking chair is a wonderful addition to your seating. It need not mean "shabby chic" – not all vintage pieces are battered and worn – but a nod to times past will often make a room feel more heart-warming.

Ditching the showroom

Some people like to live in a showroom, but what are they putting on show? Their income, their class, or their divine taste and style? A showroom could instead be a gallery of the very best of you, with quirks and laughs and hugs and kindness. Let your furnishings state clearly what you are all about. A footstool shouts "put up your feet"; two chairs grouped together says "let's talk for a while"; scuffed leather sighs "I love this sofa too much to part with it"; and a marked and notched dining table shows that many people have sat and worked, drawn, eaten and chatted there.

The right stuff

Having said that, your home has grown with you, and echoes different phases of your life. You don't need to hoard things for the sake of it. Clutter can weigh you down, mentally as well as physically. Keep only the things that matter the most. Shelves full of books create a comforting vibe, but not if paperbacks are spilling on to the floor. Are you ever going to lend or reread that thriller you read on the train a year ago and moaned about because the ending was disappointing? Do you really need all those titles with wrinkled pages from reading them in the bath? The same goes for larger items: too many chairs, rugs or tables full of ornaments will overpower your space and leave it feeling claustrophobic or gloomy.

Finding balance

It is important to remember that you can't hygge the whole time. Hygge needs contrast between the rushing and concentrating and achieving, and the relaxing and reminiscing and being in the moment. Similarly, your home needs to be functional as well as reassuring. It is where your family goes about its business and as such needs to work for practical needs. That's why lighting is so vitally important. A bathroom can be transformed from a teenage girl's brightly lit operation headquarters for a big night out to a mother's refuge, with candles and shadows and steamy mirrors.

Nature's wonders

Many hygge moments take place in the great outdoors, and an appreciation of nature's wonders can bring you joy and a sense of calm. By bringing some of this living, growing beauty into your home, your home will flourish.

Green is good

There are tangible benefits to having living plants in your home. They recycle the air, use up the carbon dioxide that we all breathe out and replenish oxygen supplies. Studies also suggest that leafy plants help to filter the air in other ways. The leaves and roots absorb noxious gases that are found in many household items, including plastics, detergents, cleaning fluids, smoke, and some fabrics and cosmetics. Some plants are better at this than others; try to find a place for ferns, spider plants, aloe vera, and the wonderfully named peace lilies. Do be careful if you have pets, though, as certain houseplants are toxic to cats and dogs.

Bringing nature indoors

A stomp in the countryside is good for the soul, especially if you share it with loved ones. Taking it slowly, instead of striding out with a final destination in mind, is a more hygge-friendly way to do things. Look around you and soak up nature's glory, and stop along the way to enjoy the fresh air and the beautiful sights and smells. Harvest some pretty blooms and twigs as you go – but be cautious. Under UK law, it is illegal to pick cultivated blooms (in a park, for example) and protected rare plants such as orchids and sandwort. You can generally gather "the four Fs" – fruit, foliage, fungi and flowers – if they are for your own use and you do not uproot the whole plant.

On display

Another hygge activity is drying and preserving plants to put on display. Tie flowers in loose bunches and hang them upside down in dark, dry places to retain their colour. Make sure the flower heads do not touch each other. They should be ready to display after two or three weeks. Collect naturally dry items to go with them: seed pods, grasses, reeds and branches with cones on them. Display them in pretty vintage vases or simply in old glass jars and bottles. Remember – reusing and repurposing is a very hygge thing to do.

A splash of colour

Use natural items to brighten up your basic colour scheme. Spring flowers breathe new life into a room, although they don't tend to last for long. Carnations, dahlias, alstroemeria, chrysanthemums, calla lilies, and gladioli will all stay fresh for longer. Try adding sugar or lemonade to the water to prolong their life, and change the water every couple of days. In addition, add vodka, vinegar, crushed aspirin, or a tiny amount of bleach to kill off bacteria and keep your flowers fresh.

Fake it!

Artificial flowers have a reputation as the poor or embarrassing relatives of fresh blooms. Admittedly, they don't give off any scent and they tend to gather dust unless you clean them regularly. However, their appearance has improved drastically in recent years, and carefully chosen sprays can look authentic and pretty. Look for stems of small spring blossom, pussy willow and coin-like honesty seeds, or puffy headed armeria (sea pinks) and allium in delicate pastel shades.

Carefully arranged

In the true spirit of hygge, you can glean extra enjoyment from your flowers – fresh, dried, or artificial – before you even put them out for all to see. Take time to arrange them and appreciate their beauty along the way. Get sentimental over your favourite vase, whether it belonged to your granny or was a gift at your wedding, and experiment with flowers of varying heights. With fresh flowers, remove any leaves that will sit in the water and snip the stems diagonally at the height you need them to be. Snip off at least an inch even if they are the correct height, to allow the stems to absorb water. Begin by placing the largest flowers first, and work in layers, adding a single type of flower at a time. Keep turning the arrangement to ensure it looks good from all sides.

Show and tell

Flowers aren't nature's only bounty that you can put on display. Look for other mementoes from your outdoor adventures. Collect pretty pebbles, shells and driftwood from a trip to the coast. If you don't want them indoors, use them to decorate your garden or decking. Display pinecones and dried teasels (from the Dipsacus plant) on their own or in groups, and stockpile conkers in a large jar to show off their glorious chestnut sheen. For ultimate hygge, each item should have a story attached or a place in your heart because of the memories it rekindles.

Happy snaps

A happy home is one filled with fond memories: of relatives and friends and of times spent with favourite people. Of course, photographs are one of the best ways to relive these times. Set aside some time to sift through old pictures, on your own or in a group. Make a pot of tea or open a bottle of wine and fill your kitchen table with photo albums. It is a glorious feeling; laughing over childhood fashions and hairstyles; getting emotional about people you no longer see; reminiscing over places you visited. Have a wedding party and invite people to bring their wedding albums with them – people rarely share their wedding shots with new friends, but most people love to see them.

Sort it out

Some people are happy to scroll through digital shots on their tablet or phone, while others have reams of prints stashed away in boxes that they sift through now and then. That is hygge in itself, but you can also enjoy the process of sorting and filtering your photographs into frames and albums. Collect old frames from charity shops or invest in a large frame with multiple apertures to display your favourites. It doesn't matter whether you prefer modern frames or antique ones; the hygge is in the selection process and the feeling you get when you look at the photos each time you walk past.

The writing's on the wall

Of course, all kinds of things can be mounted on the wall to bring you joy. Many people have inspirational sayings and outpourings of love and happiness on placards and planks around the house. Gift shops and garden centres are full of hearts to hang from walls, windows and doors: wooden ones, wire ones, felt ones, ones with bells on… these are often the kind of thing to be marketed under the hygge label. They do make lovely gifts if they are given with thought and affection attached – or, even better, if you make them yourself (see page 35).

Child's play

Children give us some of the sweetest images. Make them into something to cherish by giving them pride of place: not stuck on the fridge door with a magnet, but framed and hung as part of a collection. Use your wall space to display other cherished items, too. If you aren't a fan of having nature finds scattered along windowsills, photograph them and hang them instead. Look for deep frames that can become homes to shells and stones, athletics medals or a child's first shoe. It will free up your surfaces to help with that decluttering you were aiming for.

Get crafty

For the ultimate hygge, don't go to the shops to buy your accessories. Spend time making them yourself, either alone or with a nimble-fingered friend or child. Don't worry too much if the results don't look completely professional; what matters is that you enjoyed the time spent making them.

Message board

Leave messages of love and reminders on a pretty, framed blackboard.

You will need:

Decorative frame (charity shop finds are ideal)

Glass primer

Blackboard paint

Brushes

Carefully remove the glass from the frame. Clean it to remove any grease or dirt. You may want to wear gloves to protect your hands from the sharp edges.

You will need to spray or paint the glass with primer before you can paint it. Work in a well-ventilated area and protect the surfaces underneath with newspaper. Allow the primer to dry for at least an hour.

When the glass is completely dry, apply a first coat of blackboard paint. Use strokes in a single direction; don't worry if it looks streaky, this should resolve itself as the paint dries. Leave it for another hour and check if it is dry.

Apply a second coat in the opposite direction to the first strokes.

Once it has dried, insert the glass back into the frame.

Cake stand

Nothing much beats a triangle of cake and a hot drink, but cake served on a decorative stand might just do it.

You will need:

Porcelain plate

Clear crafting glue such as E6000

Candlestick, wine glass or small bowl

Begin by testing that your items fit together satisfactorily. Turn a small, decorative bowl or a stumpy wine glass upside down to act as the pedestal, or use a candlestick standing the correct way up. The flat inner circle of your plate should fit easily over the top of the pedestal with room around the edge.

Wash the items in soapy water and dry them thoroughly. Turn the plate upside down.

Apply crafting glue around the contact surface of your pedestal item and then place it centrally on the underside of the plate.

You may want to place a weight, such as books, on to the upturned cake stand while it dries. E6000 glue dries quickly but wait a while before you turn the cake stand over, just to be sure.

Before you pack away, use a cotton bud to smear a small amount of petroleum jelly inside the lid of the glue. This should stop the tube sealing up so you can't use it again.

Height chart

Mark the passing of time with a homemade height chart. It is a guaranteed way to look back with fondness to times when your little people really were small.

You will need:

Piece of smooth timber

Sandpaper

Paints or wood stain

Brushes

Tape measure

Pencil

Permanent marker

Ruler

Number stencils (optional)

First, you need a suitable piece of wood with the correct dimensions. A piece of gravel board 150mm x 19mm will work well, or even 94mm x 8mm cladding.

Prepare the surface by sanding it and then wiping it clean.

Stain the board in the colour of your choice. You can make it coloured to match a bedroom or keep it natural.

When it has dried, lay the board flat and use a pencil to mark the measurements along one edge. Mimic a ruler and make the lines longer every 10 centimetres, and longer still every 50 centimetres. Of course, you can use feet and inches if that's what you prefer.

When you are happy that it is neat and even, go over the markings with a permanent marker. Use a short ruler to keep the lines the same length.

Hand-write the main numbers alongside the marks, or use a stencil and paint. Tape the stencils in place to ensure they don't move.

To add a personal touch, decorate the blank spaces with anything you like: handprints, photographs, dried leaves.

Use different coloured permanent pens to mark the heights of each member of the family, adding more marks every year.

Handfuls of hearts

These hearts are easy to make, with no sewing required.

You will need:

Sturdy card

Pen

Scissors

Strong glue

6cm piece of narrow ribbon

Assorted buttons

Draw heart shape onto the card in the size you require. Cut it out.

Attach the ribbon at the top of one side with glue. This is to hang the heart later.

Cover the card with a layer of buttons, using the glue to fix them in place.

Add extra buttons over any spaces. Leave it to dry and then give it a gentle shake to test that no buttons are loose.

String hearts

You will need:

Sturdy card

Pen

Scissors

Strong glue

Rough twine or string

Draw a selection of heart shapes onto the card in various sizes. Cut them out.

Place a length of twine down the centre of a solid heart, leaving 50cm above the top edge for later. Glue it onto the card.

Wind the twine over and over to cover one half of the heart, stopping when it begins to slip off the outer edge. Wind it back to the centre and out towards the other edge. Add dabs of glue to secure it as you go.

Change direction, crisscrossing the twine diagonally until the heart is completely covered.

Finish in the top centre of the heart and secure with another dab of glue. Cut the twine, leaving enough to tie in a knot and bow with the end you left loose at the start.

Make a loop with the remaining twine, for hanging, before cutting off any excess.

Clothing

There really isn't a specific hygge way to dress, regardless of what you may have seen or read about Scandinavian knitwear! Yes, chunky jumpers are great for keeping you warm outside on a winter's day but they aren't necessary if you are in front of a roaring fire or cooking in a cosy kitchen. Instead, wear whatever makes you most comfortable and is appropriate for the occasion. If you're stealing an hour to finish reading your book, you may feel more comfortable in yoga pants or even pyjamas!

Smart casual

If, however, you are intrigued by the overall style of the Danes, then think casual for most occasions. That's smart-casual when absolutely necessary, and casual-casual whenever possible.

Black and grey are the mainstays of most Danes' wardrobes, pepped up with a little silver sometimes. Clothes are well-cut and well-fitted, shoes are borderline sensible and definitely comfortable. Scarves are a must, even for men: thick, chunky ones in winter and lighter, floaty ones the rest of the time. If you can't decide which to wear, do the double – take two favourites and twist them together!

Hyggesockken

Yes, the Danish have a word for the socks worn to hygge. They aren't socks snatched at random from a drawer. They are cosy, snuggly, comfy, cuddly, thick, warm, much-loved socks that are instantly associated with downtime and daydreams and doing what you want for a while. They are just about the only prescribed clothing for hygge, but you can substitute them for favourite slippers, or bare feet in warm weather, if that's your preference.

In its place

There is one thing worth adding about clothes and hygge. It is very unhygge (uhygge in Danish) to stress about clothing because it isn't where it should be. Knowing that you want your favourite black jumper to go with those particular black trousers – yes, they're all black but they're different, and some work together better than others – can be frustrating when you simply can't find it. Make a hygge moment in itself by turning up the radio and tackling the basket of clean laundry that is waiting to be put away. And make sure that everything does have its own place. If you run out of room, you've probably got too many clothes.

Chapter 3

Hygge food

A tasty meal, a good glass of wine, a delicious dessert, even a cup of hot, strong tea: they all nourish far more than in a purely nutritional sense. Food fuels our bodies, but the act of eating can be a delight, even a ritual, that brings people together. Meals can be special occasions in their own right, and often form the basis of a family celebration. A simple get-together over coffee and cake can lift the spirits immensely. Bread, biscuits, and cake are all very hyggelig when shared with a friend, which is why so many books include recipes for these hygge staples.

Feeling better

Eating and exercising trigger the release of certain chemicals in your body that give you a feeling of pleasure or reward. Exercise stimulates serotonin, which is a natural mood stabiliser, and helps to counteract depression as well as improve the body's ability to sleep, eat and digest food. Serotonin levels are also boosted by carbohydrates, which explains why cake and pastries seem like a remedy for life's small troubles. For maximum impact, meet a friend for a walk in the park followed by a trip to your favourite café.

Happy hormones

Eating certain foods boosts dopamine, a neurotransmitter that can stimulate feelings of wellbeing and counteract fatigue and mood swings. These foods include eggs, apples, chocolate, almonds, coffee, and sesame and pumpkin seeds – all of which lend themselves to a spot of home baking and a hot drink. Spending time with people you love stimulates oxytocin, sometimes nicknamed the love hormone, which helps you to relax and has an uplifting effect on your emotions. A cuddle from a friend, ten minutes playing with your children, or simply stroking a pet will all make you feel better because of the oxytocin that is released.

Hygge and cake

Hygge has become intrinsically linked with cake – in the media and hence in people's mind's eye. As you have already read, it is about so much more than that. A simple message of 'Cake next Wednesday?' from a friend speaks volumes. It is an invitation to skip responsibility for an hour, consume confectionary that is 'naughty' but not over-indulgent, and giggle like children… And that's how it should be, every once in a while.

Take your time

The most hygge way to enjoy anything is to do it slowly and deliberately, savouring the moment, and that applies to food more than anything else. It's not just the eating but the preparation that should engage your attention for more than just a moment. A hygge home is one that is often filled with tantalising smells from the oven. But you shouldn't be a martyr or a slave to your culinary cause. Huffing and puffing alone in the kitchen is not hygge, but sharing the process with others is. That might be a spot of baking with your children, or chatting with your partner while you both potter over that night's meal, or inviting round the masses and sharing the load.

Preparing together

Take the stress out of social gatherings by making the preparation an event in itself. Invite your guests to come over early and bring their own selection of foods to cook. Open a bottle of wine and let everybody chop and chat together, stirring someone else's dish as they pass ingredients. There will be more hands to set the table, clear the kitchen, and wash the dishes, and the whole time should be filled with laughter and conversation. It's a far cry from a formal dinner party, but a lot less stressful for the hosts. It should counteract any entertaining stress you might be feeling, too.

Memories in a jar

Pickling and preserving are a wonderful way to capture memories and keep them on your shelves, quite literally. Start the process by taking a walk and gathering fruit from the

hedgerows ready to make jam or sloe gin (see chapter 5). Or visit the market and see which vegetables are in season to make chutney and pickles. If you are lucky enough to have an allotment or vegetable patch (or a friend with excess produce) then harvest the ripe vegetables and spend an afternoon in the kitchen with your favourite recipes bubbling on the hob. Each time you twist the lid off one of your concoctions, you will smile at the recollection of how they were produced.

Batch cooking

There is also something deeply satisfying about cooking way too much of something so that you can keep some for later and save yourself a task another day. Soup is very hygge – all that chopping and stirring and slow simmering – but make it even more so by finding the biggest pan you own and doubling or quadrupling the recipe. The same goes for homemade granola; it spreads a divine aroma through the house and you may as well make as much as you can in one go, because you need to keep a constant eye on it while it slowly toasts.

"After a good dinner one can forgive anybody, even one's own relations"
— Oscar Wilde

Eating en masse

A cake devoured in private can be a guilty secret, but a cake shared with friends is a gift and a joy. As the dieter's saying goes: your calories don't count if anyone eating alongside has consumed more than you have! Eating together is very important for hygge, whether you're entertaining at home, dining out or cooking around a campfire. Dining out can be a tricky concept, as the mood may just not be hygge enough for your particular group. There has been a rise in seasonal restaurants, serving sustainable food that changes depending on what is at the market that day, and they usually serve this food in an informal setting that allows you to laugh loudly and pull up another chair without upsetting your fellow diners.

> **Trending now**
>
> Hygge isn't the only life-enhancing concept in the news right now. There are other trends that can help you on your way. One such is the return to rustic cookery. No one will judge you for serving stew that has been in the slow cooker since morning, and they will happily mop up the gravy with a hearty chunk of bread. Imperfect icing is also in vogue, and you should make it your friend. Drizzle cakes, drip cakes, naked cakes and patchy, rough icing all allow you to bake your best and then stop worrying about what it looks like.

Home sweet home

Entertaining at home is generally much more hygge. It is important to remember that you, as host, are supposed to be enjoying yourself as much as everyone else. That's why it is important to invite them to help you with the preparation as well as the consumption of the food. Ask your guests to put away their phones so that everyone is "present" and "engaged". When you sit and eat together you should savour the moment as much as the food. Stack the empty dishes and leave the washing up while you catch up on tales of travel and people, and leave politics and the big topics at the door.

Family values

While it can be hard to eat together as a family or with friends every night of the week, you should aim to do so as often as possible. Make a point of inviting over grandparents or aunts and uncles at the weekend, so that your children can spend time with their extended family. Eat together and then play together. Even if you aren't a fan of board games, there must be something that brings you closer, whether it is quizzes, charades or telling stories and jokes.

Healthy hygge

These days, everyone eats but not everyone cooks. It's easy to grab a sandwich on the go or pop a pre-prepared chicken in the oven and microwave some mash. The media is full of stories about high levels of salt, sugar, and fats in processed foods, so it's hard to claim ignorance about how bad they are. Hygge decries all of this instant-food gratification, and seeks to slow things right down. The result is a much healthier diet of foods you have prepared from scratch. You don't have to spend hours in the kitchen, but the food can spend hours in the oven or slow cooker. That frees your time to carry on with work, chores, or simply enjoying yourself.

Slow cooking

One-pot dishes are a busy person's best friend. Baked or slow-cooked main courses can be prepared ahead of time and left to their own devices, gradually releasing their special aromas to greet you as you walk through the front door. Many traditional dishes – both Danish and British – can be cooked in this way. Top of the Danes' favourites are roast pork with crackling, which can be easy to prepare and is heartily appreciated by the diners. Other classics are seafood stew and fish soup, made with fresh ingredients from the ocean. A whole salmon is simple but feeds many hungry mouths. The British have their equivalents of fish pie, cottage pie, cobbler, stew and dumplings, casseroles and roasted vegetables, all of which can be thrown together reasonably quickly and then savoured much later.

When tomorrow comes

Several of these dishes have the added bonus that they taste even better after standing overnight. Chilli, curry, meatloaf and ragu are infinitely tastier eaten a day later. Any food that has aromatic base ingredients, such as onions, tomatoes, garlic, peppers, and herbs and spices, will benefit from an improved flavour as the chemical reactions initiated by cooking continue to take place. It's another reason to cook in volume and then reap the rewards a day later when you don't have to deliberate over what's on the menu.

Leftover lovelies

Many countries have a dish that uses up leftovers from the day before: colcannon, bubble and squeak, rumbledethumps, or hash. The Danes are no exception, and theirs is called biksemad (mixed food); the Swedes, too, like to throw everything in a pan and call it just that – pyttipanna, or pieces in a pan. Enjoy it as a leisurely breakfast with an egg on top, a cup of freshly brewed coffee and the newspaper.

Speedy sometimes

You can't hygge when you're in a hurry, but you can get a food fix from things that don't take all day to cook. Scones are so speedy to bake that a friend of mine rustles up a batch before school starts in the morning. You can assemble a cheese board in minutes, and then pick away at it all evening in the company of friends. Chocolate fridge cake or tiffin doesn't need you to turn on the oven, but is oh-so-satisfying as you relish each mouthful. Popcorn is a true hygge snack for movie night (but do make your own in a pan, not a microwave bag). All of these things are fast food with slow-release satisfaction.

A simple snack?

Danish rye bread forms the basis of a ubiquitous snack, the smørrebrød, or open sandwich. However, it is a far cry from a smattering of grated cheese between slices of limp bread. Smørrebrød can be miniature works of culinary art, topped with healthy choices such as smoked salmon, prawns, mackerel or herring – or not-so-healthy cured meats, mayonnaise or pork-liver paste. In true hygge style, they aren't eaten on the move, but with a knife and fork. In company, dishes of sliced breads and numerous toppings are passed around the table for everyone to share.

A baker's oven

Baking your own bread is not only hygge, but healthy. You can be certain that the ingredients are good and basic, with no hidden extras. Modern mass-produced loaves are made with the Chorleywood Process to yield more bread in a shorter amount of time. The results are lacklustre loaves with more chemicals and less taste. Bread-making needs to take time and energy. Yeast is a very hygge ingredient because it needs warmth, food and time to work its magic. Use the kneading process as thinking time, and your own release for the day's stresses. If you don't have the time to bake, choose artisan loaves and enjoy the feeling of ripping into its fresh crustiness.

Pass it on

The joy of baking can surpass the pleasures of eating. That's worth remembering if you are watching what you eat. Your feelings of hygge can stem from providing for others rather than partaking of it yourself. Really enjoy the process of weighing, mixing and waiting, and savour the smell rather than the taste. Then pop your baked goods into a tin and take them with you when you visit a friend or relative, or surprise your work colleagues with a treat.

Eating outside

The Danish make a point of spending whole days with a group of friends, starting with a leisurely breakfast and heading out for a walk, or meeting for lunch at the beach and staying until the sun goes down. While it may seem difficult to schedule in a busy life, the benefits are immense. Time spent in the sunshine boosts vitamin D, which keeps your bones, muscles, and teeth healthy and can help to fight depression. Try to eat outdoors when the weather allows it, even if it's just a dinner à deux on a Tuesday night. Food tastes great in the fresh air!

Pack up a picnic

There is something very liberating about eating without plates and cutlery, or chairs and a table. Children are free to run around as soon as they have eaten, while the adults can kick off their shoes and feel the sun on their skin. The chance to be outdoors together is too good to miss, and time spent preparing a foodie feast to pack into small containers seems like time wasted. Besides, there is so little evening left once you're home that supper is usually salad or an omelette, so things balance out in the end.

Danish summers

Summers in Denmark are short, so people grab every opportunity to relish the long, balmy evenings. Hordes of people gather at a long table by the lakeside to share food, drinks, songs and chatter. But you don't need a summer lodge or log cabin to be outdoors. A long table and seating for everyone is lovely but not essential. In fact, the British barbecue is the equivalent, with people perched on garden walls and deckchairs, balancing a plate on their knee. It is also an unspoken but accepted rule that everyone chips in with their own food, and lends a hand with the cooking and clearing up.

> **Down tools**
>
> If you really want to benefit from hygge, take it into the workplace. Promise yourself that you will stop for lunch and move away from your desk. Round up a few colleagues and find somewhere sunny to sit and eat together. Once again, the act of eating together will break down barriers and help you to appreciate each other. If the weather is shocking, find a quiet corner or a meeting room. You may even find that people want to share their food as well as their time, and you can all bring in cakes or treats to celebrate the end of another working week.

Comfort foods

Everyone has their own food that brings back good memories or keeps them going when they are down in the dumps. These comfort foods are often the kind you can pile on a piece of toast or eat with a spoon from a bowl, as you gaze out of the window or watch a cherished movie. They don't have to be unhealthy to make you feel cosseted; try porridge, mashed avocado, sardines or grilled cheese on toast, risotto, noodles, macaroni cheese, rice pudding or bananas and custard.

Happy days

Certain smells trigger memories, taking us back to happy times. The brain receives olfactory information via two separate areas that are linked to emotions and memory making: the amygdala and hippocampus. These are bypassed by the other senses, making smells highly emotive. Strawberries are the scent of summer, hot doughnuts hark back to the beach, and hot dogs and onions might be a date at the fairground or a football match. Research suggests that associations between food and happy times make food taste better as well as boosting our mood.

Carbohydrate comforts

The common ingredient in many comfort foods is carbohydrates. The Danes love them, but do tend to get them from different sources to the Brits. While the British fill up on bread and pasta – sometimes wholemeal, not always – Danish cooks serve many more potatoes, which contain unrefined starch so retain more of their nutrients. Cooked with the skins on, potatoes also keep their vitamin C and provide healthy fibre. Danish bread is a very different from British bread, too. The Danes thrive on sour-dough rye bread, which is much higher in fibre and easier to digest than bread made with wheat, as the long fermentation time breaks down the glutens.

Hygge not huge

You may now be asking how all this hygge doesn't make people incredibly overweight. There is a lot of talk about cake and comfort foods. Here's the thing: hygge is about contrast and appreciating the good times when they pop up unannounced. Cakes and such like are intended as treats, which by their very definition are things you don't have often. Hygge isn't achieved by eating whatever you want, whenever you want it. Instead, really enjoy those precious moments when you indulge. A piece of cake is not hyggelig if you devour it without taking notice of the tastes, smells and textures on your tongue. Then, it's just empty calories.

Dairy-free Chia Granola Pots

SERVES: 6

50 ml / 1 ¾ fl. oz / ¼ cup runny honey

600 ml / 1 pint / 2 ½ cups soya milk

100 g / 3 ½ oz / ½ cup chia seeds

75 ml / 2 ½ fl. oz / ¼ cup maple syrup

75 ml / 2 ½ fl. oz / ¼ cup apple juice

1 tbsp extra virgin olive oil

175 g / 6 oz / 1 ¾ cups rolled buckwheat flakes

100 g / 3 ½ oz / ¾ cup walnuts, chopped

150 g / 5 ½ oz / 1 cup blueberries

Dissolve the honey in the soya milk, then stir in the chia seeds. Cover and chill in the fridge for 4 hours or ideally overnight.

Preheat the oven to 160°C (140°C fan) / 325F / gas 3.

Stir the maple syrup, apple juice and oil together in a bowl with a pinch of salt then toss it with the buckwheat flakes and walnuts.

Spread out the mixture on a large baking tray and bake for 1 hour, stirring every 10 minutes to ensure it all toasts evenly. Leave the granola to cool completely, then store in an airtight jar.

When you're ready to serve, spoon a little granola into the bottom of six small glasses or jars. Stir the chia mixture and spoon it on top, then add a little more granola and top with blueberries.

Prep time: 15 minutes

Cooking time: 1 hour

Chilling time: 4 hours

Chocolate and Cherry Crepes

SERVES: 4

250 g / 9 oz / 1 cup canned cherries in syrup

1 tbsp kirsch

2 tsp cornflour (cornstarch)

150 g / 5 ½ oz / 1 cup plain (all-purpose) flour

2 tbsp icing (superfine) sugar

2 tbsp unsweetened cocoa powder

1 large egg

350 ml / 12 ½ fl. oz / 1 ½ cups whole milk

1 tbsp butter

Heat the cherries and their syrup in a small saucepan with the kirsch. Slake the cornflour with 1 tablespoon of cold water. When the cherry syrup starts to simmer, stir in the cornflour. Stir over a medium heat until the sauce boils and thickens. Set aside in a warm place.

Sieve the flour, icing sugar and cocoa into a bowl and make a well in the centre. Break in the egg and pour in the milk then use a whisk to gradually incorporate all of the flour from round the outside.

Melt the butter in a medium frying pan then whisk it into the batter.

Put the buttered frying pan back over a low heat. Add a small ladle of batter and swirl the pan to coat the bottom.

When it starts to dry and curl up at the edges, turn the crepe over with a spatula and cook the other side until cooked through.

Repeat with the rest of the mixture then serve the crepes with the warm cherry sauce.

Preparation time: 15 minutes

Cooking time: 20 minutes

Blueberry and Walnut Muffins

MAKES: 12

1 large egg

120 ml / 4 fl. oz / ½ cup sunflower oil

2 tbsp orange juice

120 ml / 4 fl. oz / ½ cup milk

375 g / 12 ½ oz / 2 ½ cups self-raising flour, sifted

1 tsp baking powder

200 g / 7 oz / ¾ cup caster (superfine) sugar

150 g / 5 oz / 1 cup blueberries, plus extra to garnish

50 g / 1 ¾ oz / ½ cup walnuts, chopped

1 orange, zest finely grated

Preheat the oven to 180°C (160°C fan) / 350F / gas 4 and line a 12-hole muffin tin with cases.

Beat the egg in a jug with the oil, orange juice and milk until well mixed.

Mix the flour, baking powder, sugar, blueberries, walnuts and orange zest in a bowl, then pour in the egg mixture and stir just enough to combine.

Divide the mixture between the cases, then bake in the oven for 20 minutes. Test with a wooden toothpick, if it comes out clean, the cakes are done. If not, test again in 5 minutes.

Transfer the cakes to a wire rack and leave to cool completely, then garnish with blueberries.

Prep time: 25 minutes

Cooking time: 20 minutes

Chocolate Coconut Truffles

MAKES: 24

For the ganache

225 ml / 8 fl. oz / ¾ cup canned coconut milk

300 g / 10 ½ oz / 2 cups dark chocolate (min. 85% cocoa solids), finely chopped

2 tbsp coconut oil

To decorate

200 g / 7 oz / 1 ¼ cups dark chocolate (min. 85% cocoa solids), finely chopped

28 g / 1 oz / ¼ cup desiccated coconut

Put the coconut milk in a small saucepan with a pinch of salt and heat it gently. Meanwhile, put the chocolate and coconut oil in a mixing bowl.

When the coconut milk starts to simmer, pour it over the chocolate in the bowl. Leave it to stand for 30 seconds, then stir gently until it forms a homogenous smooth ganache.

Cover with cling film and chill for 4 hours or until fully set.

Roll heaped teaspoons of the mixture into balls and spread them out on a plate. Chill the ganache balls in the fridge for at least 30 minutes

To decorate, melt the chocolate in a bain-marie or the microwave. Dip each ganache ball in melted chocolate and transfer to a sheet of greaseproof paper. Sprinkle with a little desiccated coconut then leave to set.

Prep time: 45 minutes

Cooking time: 5 minutes

Chilling time: 4 hours 30 minutes

Chocolate Mug Cakes

MAKES: 2

55 g / 2 oz / 1/4 cup butter, softened

55 g / 2 oz / 1/4 cup caster (superfine) sugar

1 large egg

55 g / 2 oz / 1/3 cup self-raising flour, sifted

1 tbsp cocoa powder

50 g / 1 ¾ oz / 1/3 cup dark chocolate (min. 60% cocoa solids), chopped

2 tbsp double (heavy) cream

1 tbsp dark and white chocolate chips

Beat the butter and sugar together in a mug until pale and smooth.

Break the egg into a second mug and beat gently with a fork, then gradually stir the egg into the butter mixture.

Fold in the flour and cocoa powder, followed by 1 tablespoon of the chopped chocolate, then spoon half of the mixture into the mug you used to beat the egg and level the tops.

Transfer the mugs to a microwave and cook on full power for 1 minute 30 seconds. Test the cakes by inserting a skewer into the centre – if it comes out clean, they're ready. If not, return to the microwave for 15 seconds and test again.

In a separate mug, put the rest of the chopped chocolate and the cream. Cook on medium powder for 20 seconds and stir, then return to the microwave, checking every 10 seconds until the chocolate has melted. Stir until smooth, then drizzle over the cakes and decorate with chocolate chips.

Preparation time: 15 minutes

Cooking time: 2 minutes

Lamb Hotpot

SERVES: 6

1 kg / 2 lb 3 ½ oz / 7 cups boneless lamb neck, cubed

2 tbsp olive oil

1 onion, chopped

2 carrots, peeled and cut into chunks

2 sticks celery, cut into chunks

6 sprigs fresh thyme

1 tbsp plain (all-purpose) flour

800 ml / 1 pint 7 fl. oz / 3 ¼ cups lamb or chicken stock

1 kg / 2 lb 3 ½ oz potatoes

Preheat the oven to 160°C (140° fan) / 325F / gas 3.

Blot the lamb with kitchen paper to ensure it is completely dry then season liberally with salt and pepper. Heat the oil in a frying pan over a high heat then sear the lamb in batches until browned all over.

Remove the meat from the pan, lower the heat a little and add the onions, carrots, celery and thyme. Cook for 10 minutes, stirring occasionally until softened.

Increase the heat and stir in the flour then incorporate the stock and bring to a simmer. Arrange the lamb in a casserole dish and pour over the stock and vegetables.

Slice the potatoes 5 mm (¼ in) thick with a sharp knife or mandolin and arrange them on top of the lamb.

Cover the dish tightly with foil or a lid. Bake for 2 hours 30 minutes, then remove the foil and bake for another 30 minutes to colour the top.

Preparation time: 25 minutes

Cooking time: 3 hours

Toffee Popcorn

SERVES: 4

50 g / 1 ¾ oz / ¼ cup butter

100 g / 3 ½ oz / ½ cup dried sweetcorn kernels

For the toffee:

50 g / 1 ¾ oz / ¼ cup butter

50 g / 1 ¾ oz / ¼ cup light muscovado sugar

50 g / 1 ¾ oz / ¼ cup golden syrup

Preheat the oven to 180°C (160°C fan) / 350F / gas 4 and line a baking tray with a non-stick baking mat.

Melt the butter in a heavy-based saucepan over a medium heat. Add a small pinch of corn kernels and wait for them to pop, then add the rest of the kernels and shake the pan to level.

Cover the pan and take it off the heat for 30 seconds. Put the pan back over the heat and cook until the sound of popping slows to one pop every 3 or 4 seconds, shaking the pan gently. Tip the popcorn into a large bowl and set aside.

To make the toffee, put the butter, sugar and golden syrup in a saucepan. Stir over a low heat until the sugar dissolves, then bring to a simmer.

Pour the toffee over the popcorn and toss to coat. Spread the popcorn out on the prepared baking tray, then toast in the oven for 4 minutes.

Leave to cool to room temperature, then break into pieces and serve.

Preparation time: 10 minutes

Cooking time: 10 minutes

Pea and Bacon Soup

SERVES: 4

- 2 tbsp olive oil
- 2 tbsp butter
- 1 onion, finely chopped
- 2 cloves of garlic, crushed
- 100 g / 3 ½ oz / ½ cup dried green split peas
- 1 litre / 1 pint 15 fl. oz / 4 cups fresh vegetable stock
- 300 g / 10 ½ oz / 2 cups garden peas, defrosted if frozen
- 1 tbsp flat leaf parsley, chopped
- 6 rashers dry-cure streaky bacon, chopped
- 2 tbsp Greek yogurt

Heat the oil and butter in a saucepan and fry the onion for 5 minutes or until softened.

Add the garlic and split peas to the pan and cook for 2 more minutes, then stir in the vegetable stock.

Simmer for 45 minutes or until the split peas are starting to break down, then add the garden peas and parsley.

Blend the soup until smooth with an emersion blender or in a liquidizer then taste and adjust the seasoning with salt and pepper.

Dry fry the bacon in a hot pan until golden and crisp, then stir two thirds of it into the soup.

Ladle into four warm bowls and garnish with Greek yogurt and the rest of the bacon.

Preparation time: 10 minutes
Cooking time: 1 hour

Pumpkin Cupcakes

MAKES: 12

- 150 g / 5 oz pumpkin, sliced
- 150 g / 5 oz / 1 cup plain flour
- 1 tsp cinnamon
- ½ tsp ground ginger
- ½ tsp ground allspice
- 1 tbsp baking powder
- 1 tsp bicarbonate soda
- 100 g / 3 ½ oz / ½ cup butter
- 100 g / 3 ½ oz / ½ cup golden caster sugar
- 2 eggs
- 100 ml / 3 ½ fl. oz skimmed milk
- 150 g / 5 oz low fat cream cheese
- 150 g icing sugar
- 1 tsp vanilla extract
- pumpkin seeds

Preheat oven to 200°C (180°C fan) / 400F / gas 6 and place the sliced pumpkin into the oven for 20 minutes until soft. Remove and when cooled remove the flesh and blend into a puree in a food processor or blender.

Place 12 muffin cases into a muffin tin, or lightly grease a muffin tin. Combine the flour, spices, baking powder and bicarbonate of soda in a large mixing bowl.

In a separate bowl, combine half the butter and sugar, beat together until light and fluffy. Add the eggs, one at a time, and mix. Stir in the milk and pumpkin puree using a wooden spoon, followed by the flour mixture.

Spoon the mixture into the muffin cases and bake for 30 minutes until light and bouncy. Cool in the tin before removing to a wire rack.

Combine the cream cheese and remaining butter and beat until smooth. Gradually add the icing sugar then vanilla extract and mix until light. Ice the cakes once cooled and sprinkle over some pumpkin seeds.

Preparation time: 20 mins

Cooking time: 1 hr

Mint Shake

SERVES 1

1 ½ shots dark crème de cacao

1 shot white crème de menthe

1 shot Irish cream liqueur

1 tbsp unsweetened cocoa powder

2 scoops dark chocolate ice cream

4 ice cubes

TO SERVE

whipped cream

1 tbsp mint chocolate sauce

Measure the crème de cacao, crème de menthe and Irish cream liqueur into a liquidizer.

Add the cocoa, ice cream and ice cubes and blend for 30 seconds or until very smooth.

Pour the shake into a glass and garnish with whipped cream and mint chocolate sauce.

Parmesan Pumpkin Bake

SERVES: 4

1 small butternut squash, peeled and cubed

2 tbsp olive oil

1 tbsp fresh thyme leaves

600 ml / 1 pint / 2 ½ cups milk

400 g / 14 oz / 4 cups dried macaroni

2 tbsp butter

1 ½ tbsp plain flour

150 g / 5 ½ oz / 1 ½ cups Cheddar cheese, grated

Preheat the oven to 190°C (170°C fan) / 375F / gas 5.

Toss the squash with the oil and thyme and season with salt and pepper. Spread it out in a large roasting tin and roast for 30 minutes, turning halfway through.

Transfer the squash to a liquidizer and blend with the milk until smooth.

Cook the macaroni in boiling, salted water for 10 minutes or until almost cooked. Drain well.

Meanwhile, pour the squash milk into a saucepan and add the butter and flour. Stir over a medium heat until it thickens and starts to simmer.

Take the pan off the heat and stir in the cheese. Stir in the macaroni and scrape it into a baking dish.

Bake for 45 minutes or until the top is golden brown and the pasta is cooked.

Preparation time: 20 mins

Cooking time: 45 mins

Hygge food

Chapter 4

Hygge activities

Some things have essence of hygge running right through them. Snuggly socks, cake, candles... you have already heard plenty about them. But what about hygge things to do? Hygge, the Scandinavian way, often involves snow, log cabins and skiing, but there are other essentially Scandinavian ways to spend your time that don't require repatriation. Begin by heading outside and breathing fresh air. Then, get ready to be active.

Water babies

The thrill of canoeing on an open river might not seem hygge at first, but it can be. The first paddle strokes transport you into another world, and as the current takes you, you will most certainly be focussing wholly on the here and now. If that's not for you, a more gentle paddle across a calm lake allows more time for reflection and being in the moment. It's a great way to find solitude, if that's what you need after a busy week.

Messing about on the water

Paddling may be very Scandinavian but there are British equivalents that are equally hygge. Many happy memories stem from family fun in a pedalo on a boating lake. If the pedalo is shaped like a swan, or you get caught up in the vegetation at the side of the lake, it's even more memorable! Rowing boats are also great fun in a group. Whether you're the one romantically trailing your hand through the water as someone else does the hard work, or seated in a pair trying to coordinate your strokes so you don't spin round in circles, you will relax and unwind as you leave the land behind you. If even that is too much like hard work, you could hire a day boat with friends. Throw in a picnic and some rugs and set sail on a new adventure!

On dry land

Not all Scandinavians take to the water for their hygge moments. Trekking and hiking are common pastimes, and cycling is just as popular. Going for a wander after a busy day may not raise your heart rate, but it will definitely soothe your spirit. The Danes will walk and cycle however cold it is, but Brits do have to deal with some very wet, miserable conditions. Just remember the advice: there is no such thing as bad weather, only bad clothing. Wrap up well, ensure you're wearing something waterproof, and step out in your wellies or walking boots. If you want to get fitter, try Nordic walking with poles – it engages your upper body as well as your legs, and uses a lot more energy.

The best of British

The UK has a wealth of beauty and is small enough that most people live only a car journey or train ride away from the open countryside or the coast. Seek out its Areas of Outstanding Natural Beauty (AONB) and you will begin to understand how lucky we are. There are more than 40 designated AONB covering a little under one-fifth of the UK and they include open moorland, heaths and forests, rocky outcrops and hills, as well as valleys. If you prefer something a little more cultivated, spend an afternoon at one of the hundreds of historic houses and gardens protected by the National Trust. Immerse yourself in the nation's history at English Heritage sites, such as Hadrian's Wall, Stonehenge and Lindisfarne Island. Hygge may be about being in the moment, but steeping yourself in our colourful past is a great way to find it.

Fun in the sun

If your hygge can be found in a crowd, then a festival provides the backdrop to lose yourself entirely. Many festival memories, however hazy, involve strangers who became your best friends for an afternoon. The Brits are not the only nation to watch live music in the open air, but they have become particularly good at enjoying it regardless of wind and rain. If music festivals don't appeal to you, there are many food festivals, religious festivals, well-being festivals, and art festivals to tempt you into a field full of like-minded people.

A home from home

There are other typically British pastimes that can bring a smile to your face. While continental Europeans have a café culture, we have the pub. Whether it's your destination after a winter walk to shed your outer layers in front of a huge roaring fire, or a meeting place in summer to do a spot of "beer gardening" on an unexpectedly sunny day, the pub is a great place to eat, drink, and chat in relaxed surroundings. Away from the house, you can forget about the chores waiting for you. At the pub, there is still that feeling of homeliness, as no one stands on ceremony or lingers in the hope that you will hurry up and leave your table free for someone else. While the drinks and food are flowing, you are welcome to stay as long as you like.

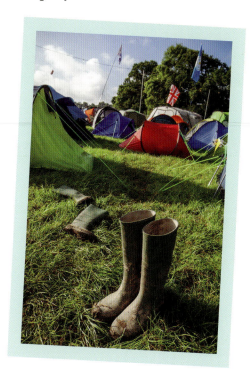

Double hygge

If you're planning a full day with friends, you will need to mix it up a little or the moments will pass and the feeling will be lost. Staying indoors from morning until bedtime, even if you're surrounded by your favourite people, will lack the charm and the buzz of a truly hyggelig time. Head out of the house for at least some of the time, whatever the weather. Join your children for a snowball fight or have a snowman-building competition. Splash through puddles and kick up the leaves on a country lane or in the park. Work up an appetite, feel the flush in your cheeks, and then head back home to get warm and dry.

The great indoors

After your jaunt outside, you can settle in for some lazy time, with popcorn and feel-good films. Watch tried-and-trusted movies that you've seen before. You shouldn't have to worry if a conversation starts up and makes you miss a scene, or you keep pressing the pause button while people top up their hot chocolate or mulled wine. Let the children have their own downtime, too. These days, checking their social media and catching up online are just as important to them as cosy get-togethers are to adults. Again, it's all about the contrast; they will become bored and twitchy if you insist they remain cuddled up on the sofa next to you for hours on end. Just make it clear that they will be expected to join you for food and entertainment again later.

Feeding the masses

Your hygge day will undoubtedly be filled with food. Make the shopping part of the activities; head to a food market and choose your favourite things to share, or encourage the youngsters to lead the way down the supermarket aisles and find something that is tasty and nutritious. Make sure they help when you arrive home by unloading the car and putting things away. As always with hygge, no one should be doing the jobs alone. Even the youngest in a group can be given a simple task.

Me time

How do you hygge? When it is just you – solely you – you have the place to yourself and the choice to do anything you want? Times like these can be overwhelming as you look at your to-do list and can't decide where to start. Begin by getting some important tasks out of the way. Achieving small goals and ticking off tasks increases your dopamine levels and makes you feel even more motivated. Then you can reap the rewards of your happier state as you take a little time for yourself.

Hygge hobbies

Many solo activities involve focus and concentration. Reading, doing puzzles, colouring books, knitting, painting, sewing: they all channel the mind and make you tune out the background noise of other jobs that you could be doing. Yoga and meditation require you to zone in on your body and how you are feeling. Make the most of this me-time and don't allow anyone to make you feel guilty for it. You don't even have to actively do anything to grab a hygge moment. Allow your mind to wander and your eyes to unfocus; stare out of the window at the snow falling or the rain tracing patterns down the glass; daydream or cloud-watch or fire-gaze or even take a nap. Your body and spirits will benefit.

Slow down

It is hard to hygge if you are stressed. Too many commitments, too much to think about, too little time to fit everything in… These all create a mental chatter that can grind you down. Learning to meditate can help to clear this mental noise and free your mind to enjoy more of life – and to achieve more with your time, too. Use your comfy corner as a meditation space – all you need is a comfortable seat or a cushion on the floor. Sit with your legs crossed or your feet planted side by side, flat on the floor. Keep your back straight, mouth closed, and eyes lowered to look at a point about a metre in front of you. Breathe slowly in and out through your nose, counting from 10 down to 1 to focus your mind.

Advanced breathing

As you learn to lose yourself in your breathing, begin to notice more about each breath. Think about how it feels as it passes through your body and into your chest. Notice how the air touches your nostrils and makes your torso fill and empty. Don't be distracted by outside sensations such as scents and sounds. Simply let your mind log them and file them away as smell or noise without trying to identify them. Practise for just one or two minutes each day and increase the length of time gradually.

Handmade hygge

If you like being surrounded by objects as reminders of times past, or to prod your thoughts towards the simple pleasures, then try making items yourself. As you know, there's hygge to be had in the process of creating something. If that really is beyond your skillset or not a way for you to enjoy yourself, then consider paying someone else to do so. Homemade and handmade possessions counteract the soulless production line items that can be picked up anywhere. Spend a morning wandering around a gallery or craft fair to find individual pieces and meet the people who made them.

Savvy shopping

Selective shopping is important to feeling good inside. Don't line the pockets of the big money-men with every purchase. When you can, cycle to a farm shop or your local butcher and chat with the shopkeeper. Ask advice on the best cuts of meat, or what to do with seasonal vegetables, and find out more about the provenance of the foods you're purchasing. The world is not a better place because we can shop in store or online 24/7. It encourages consumerism and, at the supply end, often poor working conditions and low pay. Shop ethically whenever you can, and keep your online shopping to a weekly grocery order that frees up your time to be used enjoyably elsewhere.

Buy less, borrow more

Buying less and borrowing more is a very sociable and socially-aware way to consume less. Call round to see if a neighbour has the equipment you need for a DIY project or a bumper cooking day before you purchase items you might use only twice a year. Stop for a cup of tea and discuss the project first; they might have some tips and advice. Of course, when you return their belongings, make sure they're in tiptop condition and accompanied by a little thank you cake or a bottle of wine, and the offer to return the favour if you can ever help.

Reusing

If you can't borrow an item, can you buy it second hand? Redistributing items is so much better than throwing them into landfill. Learning how to repair items or redeploy them is satisfying. That cast-iron wok with a broken handle could become a cactus garden, and a disused washing basin can be part-buried in the ground to keep mint under control. Hygge may come from looking back with fondness and enjoying the here and now, but it can also happen when you take care of the future by nurturing our planet. Give something back and you will turn your hygge into superhygge!

Chapter 5

Hygge through the seasons

From spring and summer through to autumn and winter, there are hyggelig moments to savour throughout the year.

Spring

Spring really is the time to take notice of nature. After the gloom of winter, everything begins to burst into life. Some of my favourite hygge moments occur on those spring days when the weather turns a corner and is fine enough to hang the washing on the line. Relish the warmth, and steal an extra five minutes in the garden. Let the sun soak into your skin, and notice the branches breaking into bud and spring bulbs blooming with colour. Breathe deeply and listen to the chirrup of the birds.

Bee happy

Early bees go about their business at this time of year. There are more than 200 species of solitary bee in Britain, many of which nest in small cavities. These bees are a huge boon to wildlife as they pollinate even more plants than honeybees. They are friendly, non-aggressive insects that are safe around pets and children. You can encourage them into your garden in a variety of ways: hang a bee hotel in a sunny, secluded corner or plant bee-friendly flowers, such as forget-me-not, crocuses, thrift and primulas. Check, though, that your plants are from bee-friendly sources with no neonics or other pesticides.

Bee blue!

Bees also love bluebells, which carpet the floor of many woodland areas in spring. Take a walk in the woods for an instant boost to your spirits. Let yourself become immersed in the rustle and swish of the hidden activity at your feet, drowning out the noise of that "other life" you left at the edge of the trees. Just don't dig them up to claim a little bit of the loveliness for your own garden – it is illegal and you are likely to be fined.

Nature watch

If you are stuck at work while spring is strutting its stuff outside, then don't ignore it. Studies have shown that looking outside and admiring nature can boost your work rate, focus your attention, and improve how well you perform. Just a minute or two of gazing at the trees and hedges in bloom can help.

"Behold, the Spring has come; the earth has received the embraces of the sun and we shall soon see the results of that love! Every seed is awakened and so has all animal life. It is through this mysterious power that we too have our being, and we therefore yield to our neighbours, even our animal neighbours, the same right as ourselves, to inhabit this land"

— Sitting Bull

Burn baby burn

You might associate a crackling bonfire with autumn, but spring is a great time to burn your garden rubbish, especially if it has been a windy winter. Gather up dead leaves and debris and pile them into a chiminea or metal incinerator bin. Ensure there is no green waste or treated substances that might give off toxic fumes. Warn your neighbours beforehand; your hygge should not encroach on theirs. Spring fires are at their best as the nights draw out, wrapped up in a toasty cardigan with a mug of hot, spiced cider.

I spy

If curling up indoors is still your thing, then watch nature's spring glory unfold before you as the birds begin nesting. Settle yourself by a window and watch the birds come and go, first carrying nesting material in their beak, and later feeding their young with live food and scraps. Many garden birds build their nest in early spring, to hatch their babies in March and April. Lend them a hand by gathering tumble dryer fluff, the hair off your hairbrush, and pet fur into a mesh bag (saved from your bag of oranges) and hang it out of harm's way. While you watch, open the window a fraction and listen carefully. As well as the usual bird song, you might hear the babies calling for food, and the parents hissing to protect their young (although if you have robins, the babies also hiss to indicate that they're hungry).

Flying high

Another great spring activity is kite flying. In the UK, the kiting calendar begins in April, as the days become sunnier and the winds are less gusty. Always head for a wide, open space; the beach is great, or an open field or moor with few trees and no overhead cables. Don't worry if the wind isn't blowing hard – just a gentle breeze on your face, rustling the leaves of trees, should be enough. Turn your back to the wind, and ask your kite-flying comrade to hold the kite and walk about 30 paces downwind. He or she should hold the kite high up while you pull the line taut and the kite catches in the wind, then he or she can let go. To raise the kite higher, pull on the line, and walk carefully backwards if necessary. Keep the line taut, reeling in any slack caused by a drop in the wind. When you want to stop, reel in the line slowly to prevent tangles. If you end up fighting the kite, put the line on the ground and walk along it, winding it in as you go, to bring the kite down without hurting your hands. A word of warning: never, ever fly a kite in the rain as it becomes a lightning conductor.

Summer

Ah, summer… It is pure hygge to shed layers of clothing and let the sun warm you as you go about your daily tasks. Take a moment to sit for a while in a sunny spot and let the rays kiss your face; take your friends outside with you to share the love, or enjoy the solitude as you concentrate your attention on the live-giving beams of light.

Too tense or two tents?

If you get back to nature only once this summer, do it in a tent. Camping is the British equivalent to the log cabin: a simple life with basic amenities, where everyone pitches in together to keep people fed and the surroundings clean and tidy. There are few other settings where you can convince children that washing up is fun or showering in flip-flops is acceptable. Join forces with friends to cook together: sausages on one barbecue, burgers on another, beans on a gas ring slowly sticking to the bottom of the pan. If you are on a campsite, you can rest assured that the children are kept safe within its confines, and are probably making new friends as you relax. Drink wine as the sun sets and all the children gather in a single tent to swap stories. It is truly one of the best ways to share laughs and good times with your friends.

Go crazy

Nature walks and mountain hikes are all very fine, but sometimes there are members of the group who are less mobile, or youngsters who haven't yet been won over by the glory of nature. So how do you find a summer-day activity that suits everyone? Try a round of mini golf or crazy golf. It appeals to all ages and all sporting abilities; in fact, it can be a great leveller, with the 15-handicap enthusiast being beaten by the steady-handed teenager or the first-time lucky grandma. There is little more likely to bring joy and laughter than the big brother who can't get past the water feature, or the cocky uncle who keeps overhitting into the undergrowth.

On your bike

Studies in Scandinavia have found that cycling more than a kilometre on your commute, or cycling for at least an hour a week, can reduce the risk of developing heart disease by lowering cholesterol, blood pressure, obesity, and diabetes risks. Here in Britain, the infrastructure is only partially in place to allow more people to cycle to and from work, but there are many cycle routes to more rural destinations or places of local interest. The National Cycle Network has ten regional routes covering England, Northern Ireland, Wales, and Scotland, each dividing into branches that link towns and cities. They are mostly traffic-free paths or quiet roads; look out for the blue signs with a red route number. Pack up for a day in the saddle, with plenty of water, snacks and suntan lotion, and let your muscles and heart reap the rewards.

Dams and dens

Summer is a time of building: dams across rivers and dens in the woods. Kick off your shoes and join your children barefoot in an icy-cold stream or river to pile up rocks and stones in an attempt to stem the flow. Let them put their scientific and construction brains to the test; how would it work better? Where is the water getting through? How do you stop it pushing the small stones downriver? Once you have the basic structure in place you can probably sit on the bank and just enjoy watching them, fetching more stones and moss and working as a team. Don't forget to dismantle it before you leave – just in case their damming skills are actually quite good.

I'll huff and I'll puff

If you're nowhere near running water, build a den out of fallen branches. Usually the adults tire of this long after the little ones have become bored. There is something primal about making a shelter from the resources around you, so quitting before it's habitable is rarely an option. If you're a real hygge homemaker, you'll take great delight in seeking out tree stumps as furnishings, too.

Fire starters

Hygge is all about warmth and light, so building a campfire is one of the best summer pursuits. Crackling flames, light in the darkness: the fire is a central gathering spot, and testimony to your skills as a survivor. Ensure you are in a place that is safe for fires, and that they are not prohibited. Choose a space on sand or bare earth, with no dry plant matter. Use a branch to sweep it clear if necessary. Ring your campfire with large rocks if you like.

Get your team of helpers to gather the materials to burn. This is part of the fun, not a chore. You will need tinder to get things started: dry bark, wood shavings, even dry grass and leaves. Then pile on some kindling – small, dry twigs that will easily catch alight. Place them in a tepee shape, with a gap on the windward side to blow onto the flames once it is lit. Finally, you can add larger pieces that will burn for a while. Find pieces no bigger than your arm and pile them up around the tepee. Place a lit match under the tinder and wait for the flames to take hold. Keep a bucket of water close by for safety reasons, and when you are packing up to leave, sprinkle water onto the fire to extinguish it. Keep sprinkling, and stir through the embers with a stick, until there is no more steam or hissing noises.

Ease into a bath

By the time you have finished your work in the garden, your muscles will be shouting for mercy. Treat yourself to a soothing bath; add Epsom salts to the running water as a muscle relaxant. These mini-miracle workers can also be used to treat sunburn, remove splinters, improve sleep, detoxify, help with leg and foot cramps, and fight illnesses such as colds and flu. Light some candles and allow yourself the satisfaction of knowing you've done a good day's work.

Autumn

As the summer fades away and the leaves change colour, autumn brings a sense of muted splendour. Gone are the days when you have to worry about constantly reapplying suntan lotion and having litres of drinking water on standby. Instead, the sun sits lower in the sky and graces us only sporadically with its sparkling presence. Now is the time to cherish the last chances to head outdoors for bracing beach walks and last-chance picnics. Be wise to the weather and wear layers; a chill wind can catch you unawares, especially at the coast, but it can be surprisingly hot in the glare of the sun.

What's in store

Of course, autumn is traditionally harvest time. You should be busy in the garden, digging and picking and pruning and sowing. Potatoes, onions, apples and pears are waiting to be collected and stored for the winter. Keep potatoes in a dark place to prevent them turning green; store onions somewhere light. If you have tomatoes that are still green, pick them now and keep them in a shoebox to ripen. Trim back lavender and rosemary before the frosts bite, and use secateurs to thin out your currant and berry plants for a better crop next year. Now is also the time to prepare the ground for your next crops, and many of next year's crops can be sown now.

Autumn cleaning

You've heard of spring cleaning, but your garden and greenhouse will benefit from some autumn cleaning. Wash your greenhouse windows to allow in as much sunlight as possible. Clear the floor and shelves and disinfect all the surfaces. Remove any annual plants that are past their best and rake up any leaves that have started to fall. If you can, stockpile them to make compost and leaf mould. Survey your garden for any gaps that need filling, and plant them with evergreens and winter flowering plants such as vibrant Cotinus, vibernum, skimmia, daphnes, and white heather to cheer you up in the coming winter months.

Free gifts

Not everyone is lucky enough to have a fruitful garden or allotment. Many of us lack the time, talent or inclination to grow our own produce. That needn't mean we miss out on nature's bounty. Go foraging and see what your family can find. Autumn in Denmark is the time for mushroom picking, and there are guided tours by trained mushroom hunters to ensure you only gather mushrooms that are safe to eat. Such tours are less easy to find in the UK and it really isn't worth the risk of going it alone. However, there are plenty of fruits to be found. Blackberries grow in abundance, elderberries and their flowers are easy to find, sloes are beginning to ripen, and tiny bilberries are delicious if you are lucky enough to have them in your area. Equip the whole family with plastic containers and see who can gather the most fruit.

Fast food

The great thing about autumn fruits such as berries, apples, plums and pears is that they can quickly be turned into something delicious to eat. You can rustle up a crumble in no time, and the smell as it cooks will fill your home with hygge. For a longer-term investment, turn them into cordial, jams, and jellies, and you will unlock a memory every time you twist open the top.

Go sloe

Making sloe gin is an excellent hygge activity. It is a long but rewarding process with a delicious and slightly decadent result at the end. Sloes are quite common in Britain: they were planted to mark boundaries and so can often be found in the hedges surrounding

fields. They grow by the roadside, in woodlands, and even on wasteland in urban areas. Look for a large bush, between 1 and 4 metres tall, with slender green leaves and round purple fruit. The bush is called the blackthorn but the thorns, although about 2 centimetres long, are often hard to find. The berries are the size of a small marble with green inner flesh around a central stone, and taste incredibly bitter if eaten raw. If the fruit sucks all the moisture from your mouth, you have found your fruit! Sloes look ripe in the early autumn but should be picked after the first frost. If the frost hasn't started by November, collect the berries and freeze them before you use them.

Foraging is only the first part of the process. Next, you need to prick each berry with a needle several times and place them in a large container. Add 250 grams of caster sugar for every 500 grams of sloes, pour over a litre of gin, and then seal the container. Place the container in a dark place and wait. Shake the jar for the first few days to help the sugar to dissolve and then leave it for at least two months before you taste the drink. The longer you can bear to leave it, the better: it should take on a deep, red-brown colour and taste smooth and rich. Drink it neat as a liqueur, added to bubbly as an alternative take on a kir royale, or make it into a long drink with tonic and ice.

Winter

Winter is, for many, the most hygge season. It is when we hide ourselves away and shut out the cold and darkness. It is when candles and throws really come into their own, and Scandi clothing doesn't seem out of place in our milder climate. But don't hide away for months on end. Invite your friends to come out and play! The more the merrier when you are snowballing and snow building. See who can build the best igloo, or build a blockade and hide from the barrage of snowballs from the opposition. Then head indoors and stoke up the fire, put on some Nat King Cole, and make a large pan of mulled wine.

The good old days

Research has found that reminiscing can boost your mood and your self-esteem. However, it is easy to remember the bad times as well as the good; the brain's 'negativity bias' means that unpleasant situations and harsh words register more strongly than positive ones. So take time to dig up memories from good old days, sharing stories with friends, playing music that reminds you of decades past, dancing to cheesy songs from your youth, laughing at fashion faux pas, and reminiscing about people you no longer see.

Don't be bored, be board

It doesn't matter if you can't play outside. You can play inside instead! Board games are a great way to pull everyone together for an afternoon of family fun. They are very hyggelig if you play in teams rather than individually, and choose games that help you to find out more about each other. Having said that, some families thrive on the competition, and enjoy games of attack and strategy and chasing each other around the board. Be aware of every person's preferences; some have steady hands but a fuzzy brain, while others like to shun the limelight and take on the role of timekeeper. Hygge isn't about picking on people, but picking out their highlights.

Common scents

When you're holed up indoors, it is easy to become insular. It's only if you leave and re-enter the house that you realise that the air is stuffy, rooms are overheated, and those snuggly socks might actually have spread a certain aroma throughout your home. Throw open some windows to let in fresh air; it's one of the best smells in the world. Once you've aired the rooms, add a little winter fragrance with pine, clove, nutmeg, cinnamon, or frankincense from candles or essential oils.

Comedy store

Laughter is one of the best medicines, as the saying goes. So fight off any winter blues by finding the fun in every day. Tickle your children and let their giggles lead you to laughs of your own. Challenge each other to find a joke that actually makes you laugh out loud. Search through old photos and make an album of ones that genuinely make you smile, either at face value or because of the back story attached. Laughing has both a physical and emotional effect. It triggers muscle contractions that increase blood flow and oxygenation, and it releases endorphins to combat pain, reduce stress, and help your immune system. Best of all, it is contagious so you won't be laughing alone.

Photo fit

While you are sifting through old photos, set yourself the task of discarding any that you don't need, and putting the best ones into frames or albums. Give each family member his or her own shoebox filled with pictures, then try to identify places, people, and dates. Not only will you enjoy the task as you do it, but you will benefit in the long run, when your children have left home and you can't quite remember the name of the friend in the football photo or the girl in the front row of the school shot.

Two-time

Get crafty with your little ones to tempt them away from the television or tablet on long days indoors. Crafts don't have to be complicated to be fun if you're doing them together. Cut snowflakes from white paper and thread them into winter bunting to hang

around the room. It's an activity that wouldn't be so fulfilling on your own, but is simple and enjoyable when you're doing it side by side.

Let there be light

Counteract winter's characteristic darkness by creating your own light shows. Start small, with tealights in tiny jars as part of a miniature lysfest (light festival), surrounded by berries, pinecones and fir. Install LED light strips in an alcove or around a child's bedroom. They are inexpensive and come in white or multicolours, with a remote control so you can switch from constant light to flashing patterns. The strips are self-adhesive so simply need a smooth, flat surface to attach them to, and can be easily connected into longer lengths. They really are an easy way to transform the light in your home.

"People don't notice whether it's winter or summer when they're happy"

— Anton Chekhov

Chapter 6

Hygge Christmas

Christmas may be the most hyggelig time of the year, but it can also be hugely stressful and demanding of your time and brainpower. The best approach is to appreciate that all good things are in proportion to the amount of effort you put in, and to plan well ahead. Write down your menus, as food is a vital component of the day. Choose dishes that you can make weeks beforehand and keep in the freezer until you need them. Bake your cake after Hallowe'en, and the smell of spices and spirits will infuse your house with the smells of Christmas to get you in the mood.

RSVP

Family members are usually the backbone of a Christmas celebration, but often have to be shared, so you should make sure the relevant people know when and where they are invited. It is always good to avoid a tug of war over your in-laws. The best relatives will offer to help, so make sure you accept – a pre-prepared dish or a sous-chef on Christmas Eve are always welcome.

"The great doesn't happen through impulse alone, and is a succession of little things that are brought together"

— Vincent Van Gogh

Customize your crackers

Of course, hygge happens when it happens, but there's no harm in helping it on its way. Tailor-made crackers and table presents might sound like too much effort, but they're worth it to see the look on people's faces when they open a silly gift chosen with them in mind. It's so much better than spending a fortune on shop-bought crackers that deliver nail clippers, plastic rings and tiny packs of playing cards. Look around for silly fancy dress items to replace paper hats. They are often found cheaply in charity shops, and can be used year after year. They might even form a new family tradition, when granddad stakes his claim to the flashing antlers because he loves them so much.

When midnight comes

Traditions are immensely important at Christmas time, and every family has its own. Ours began when our children were small, and Christmas morning was a frenzy of present opening that made it hard to remember who to thank for each gift, and even harder for the adults to truly appreciate opening their small pile of presents. A session of last minute wrapping one Christmas Eve meant that we were still awake after midnight which was, we claimed, officially Christmas Day after all. So the adults handed out their gifts, toasted the event with some bubbly, and thoroughly enjoyed watching each other open one parcel at a time.

Deck the halls

One of the most enjoyable parts of the Christmas build-up is decorating the house and the tree. Many people are a tad twitchy about how good the tree looks, whether the baubles are evenly and symmetrically placed, is the tinsel too retro, what if white lights are so last year… Stop! Who is Christmas for – you and your family, hanging up fairy lights together, or the visitors who pass through your house for brief moments? Put your tinsel torment to one side and let your children run riot with their own colours or no colour scheme at all. Take time to enjoy special baubles as you unpack them, remembering where they were bought or by whom. Make sure you have festive music in the background, and then dim the lights and admire your handiwork.

Quick fix

If you prefer to do without a tree, you can still add a festive touch. A vase filled with baubles takes no time at all and little space. Add a string of tiny battery-operated lights twisted amongst the baubles. String folksy tree decorations onto twigs and pop them in a vase that usually stands empty. Thread similar decorations through their own hanging loops in a line, like a daisy chain, and hang them at the windows or on cupboard handles.

DIY Decorations

If you're feeling crafty, you can make your own two-dimensional Christmas tree to sit neatly out of the way. Collect driftwood or dry sticks in ever-decreasing lengths to fashion a conifer shape on a wall or large open frame. Hold the sticks in place with small tacks or glue, depending on your surface. Use a glue gun or sticky pads to add lightweight decorations.

The hygge touch

Christmas wouldn't be hygge without candles. But if your home is constantly filled with them all year long, you can ring the changes with a few festive touches. Tie baubles and ribbons around candle votives. Use tealights in jars as place-holders for your dinner table on the big day. Add tiny bells or wooden snowflakes to the string that holds the name tags in place. Sprinkle rock salt or Epsom salts in the base of the jar to make them more heat-resistant, and ensure that the ribbon or string is not near the flame.

It's in the bag

Don't lose your hygge over simple things like wrapping and cards. Personalise your presents in the simplest way, with ease.

All wrapped up

Brown paper lunch bags and sandwich bags are your best friend at Christmas. Eco-friendly versions are inexpensive, and can be used for all sorts of things. Buy a selection of sizes and use them for wrapping awkwardly shaped presents or, if you hate wrapping, for all of your presents if they are small enough. Fold over the top, seal with a Christmas sticker or a plain wooden clothes peg, and add a cute wooden decoration or a bauble. Don't forget to label to show who each gift is for and from.

Christmas countdown

You can use smaller bags to custom-make an advent calendar. Pop treats inside 24 bags and seal them with a sticker and the date for opening each one. The treats can be edible or decorative – a bauble with your child's name on, a photograph, hairclips and bobbles, or handmade "treat tickets" to let them off the washing up or the vacuuming for a day. Line up the advent bags in a basket or hang them on an indoor line to open every morning.

Sent with love

Design your own Christmas card and take a photograph of it. You can then send it in digital form to save money on postage, which you can donate instead to charity and feel that glow of generosity to others. Or you can print it out and send it the traditional way with a note attached. The design doesn't have to be the standard family mug shot. Photograph your tree, a decorative display, or experiment with something more creative if the mood takes you.

Collage cards

Assemble a selection of items in the shape of a Christmas tree onto craft paper or card. Play around with colours and textures; try corrugated cardboard, woodchip wallpaper or fibreboard. Arrange buttons, stars, baubles, biscuits, leaves, wooden hearts, cinnamon sticks – whatever catches your eye – in a monochrome scheme or a mixture of brights or pastels. Glue them in place when you are satisfied with how they look, as you will need to move it around to find the best lighting for your photo. Take several shots at different times of day, in a variety of places, until you are happy with the outcome.

Make your own presents

A thoughtful homemade gift makes a wonderful treat at Christmas time. They don't have to be time-consuming either.

Five Cookie Jars

You will need:

5 Clean, sterilised jars with airtight lids

375 grams plain flour

2½ teaspoons bicarbonate of soda

2½ teaspoons baking powder

375 grams soft light-brown sugar

500g chocolate chips

300 grams oats

Sweets for decoration

Large gift tags

Pen

Ribbon

Weigh out the ingredients for each jar. Into each jar you will need to add: 75 grams flour, ½ teaspoon bicarb, ½ teaspoon of baking powder, 75 grams sugar, 100 grams chocolate chips, and 60 grams oats.

Use a funnel or piping bag to pour each ingredient into the jar, in layers. Press each layer down with the end of a rolling pin or tumbler as you go.

Carefully place the decorative sweets on top. Seal the jars without disturbing the ingredients.

Write a recipe label for each jar – see below. Add your personal message on the other side. Tie around the lid with ribbon.

Recipe to copy:

Christmas Cookies

1. Preheat your oven to 200°C (fan 180°C) /Gas 5

2. Empty the jar's ingredients into a mixing bowl.

3. Add 1 egg, 1 teaspoon vanilla extract and 2 tablespoons sunflower oil to the dry ingredients and mix well to form a dough.

4. Roll the dough into balls around 3-centimetres big, and place evenly on a greased, lined baking tray.

5. Bake for 6–8 minutes until golden brown.

6. Decorate with sweets while still soft.

Bath-time treats

These little jars of Christmas fun make beautiful decorations but they can also be given as a bath-time treat for extra hygge on a winter's night.

You will need:

Clean, sterilised jars with airtight lids

Wine corks

Strong glue

Small Christmas figures

Bath salts

Turn the lid upside down so you can see the underside. Glue a wine cork to the centre and leave to dry.

Glue a Christmas figure to the top of the cork. Play around with trees, reindeer, Santa, or just pretty baubles. Leave to dry again.

Pour bath salts into the jar to about 3cm high. You can use scented bath salts if you like, but plain Epsom salts have many healing qualities.

Screw the lid in place, being careful not to dislodge the figure. Carefully turn the jar upside down and allow the salts to settle.

If the cork is still visible, turn the jar over, unscrew the lid, and add more salts. When you are happy with the first jar, you will know how full the subsequent jars should be.

Chapter 7
Family and friends

A relationship that brings hygge is a two-way route. Spending time with your loved ones can make you happy; being happy can make you a better person to spend time with, and cheers up those around you. If yours is a hyggelig family that knows how to enjoy time together and recognise moments of contentment for the jewels they are, then the chances are that will rub off on your children and friends.

Hygge parenting

Hygge is so important in child-raising that, with togetherness, it is one of the six ingredients in the parenting checklist featured in Alexander and Sandahl's best selling book *The Danish Way of Parenting*. Contented parents raise well-rounded children with every opportunity of growing into well-rounded adults. It may be an oft-repeated piece of advice, but that's because of the truth it speaks: if you want your children to flourish, spend less money on them and more time with them. It costs nothing to get out into the garden and throw a ball around, bounce on the trampoline, or even just watch as they race around while you play the role of stop-watch holder. Be open-minded and join them doing things that you would never do alone. Find the joy in things you don't enjoy, whether it is watching a sport or doing a colouring book together, if those are the activities your child chooses.

Positive words

The way you think and talk to your children has a huge impact on their outlook on life. Words of encouragement will stay with them into adulthood. Let them know that you not only love them, but also value them and enjoy their company. Listen to their ideas and tell them when you take them on board. Show interest in their opinions and acknowledge when their way of seeing things changes your views. Help them to see beyond a negative and seek out the positive. Be sure to thank them when they help you, and praise them when they do things without being asked. Above all, devote yourself wholly to them when you are spending hygge time together. Listen, laugh, get excited, immerse yourself in your together-world; stop being an adult and a parent and just enjoy your friendship for a while.

> **Hygge time**
>
> It is important to remember that you can't live your whole life in hygge. Daily tasks need completing and difficult topics need to be discussed. People have legitimate grievances with each other. Children need to be disciplined, and although there are different approaches to this, none of them is going to qualify as hyggelig. But you can and should put all those things to one side sometimes.

Social time

Hygge is, for the most part, a social thing. However, introverts need not run and hide at this point; after all, hygge is also about intimacy and trust, and is more likely to be found in a small, cosy gathering than at a large party. You will need to let down some barriers, though, and invite "outsiders" into your castle. This may involve expanding your comfort zone to include people beyond your family, or being willing to accept the invitation into another person's world. You don't have to be the most gregarious person at a gathering to contribute to the hygge. Remember, it is all about sharing the load and not hogging the limelight, which suits quieter personalities just fine.

Chit chat

Hygge gatherings are low key and comforting. Crass comments, blowing your own trumpet, and boastful remarks will all kill the mood that others have so carefully nurtured. Ask about the little things in life and quiz your friends about what they have been up to, how their parents are, and what's going on with their children. Leave the big topics for later, if you really want to discuss politics or press your friends for their views on global warming.

Surprise!

Of course, not all encounters are scheduled. Some of the best hygge moments happen when you're pottering at home and guests call round unannounced. If you aren't skilled at dealing with surprise visits, this can be unnerving. There's always the temptation to keep friends standing on the doorstep while you explain that you're in the middle of

cleaning the bathroom. But stop for a minute, and think. Can the cleaning wait? Will you get the chance to see your visitors again soon if you turn them away? How lovely would it be to peel off your rubber gloves, boil the kettle, and forget about chores for an hour? There's your answer. The toothpaste marks on the basin really aren't worth worrying about, in the grand scheme of things.

Join the club

The Danes relish time spent together, and are renowned for "joining" – they find happiness en masse, by grouping together over a shared interest or hobby. Becoming a member of your local choir, or saluting the sun together at a yoga class can deliver more enjoyment than singing alone or doing the tree pose in your own back garden. It is a great way to steal back some "you time", too. There is a sense of liberation in knowing that you have to walk out and leave the housework behind because your zumba class starts in 20 minutes, or your netball team needs you.

One-on-one

Life is often spent at extreme ends of the sociability scale. We're either surrounded by people that we work with, travel with, exercise with, celebrate with and shop with in a crush of bodies, or we shut ourselves away to think, work, meditate, read or go online alone. Sometimes, it's nice to slide just a little farther up that scale, and spend some one-on-one time with a loved one. Often, that's a partner, but it may just as easily be a child or a parent or a best friend. The act of downing tools and showing that you value a person enough to give them your time speaks volumes.

Date night

Taking time to be alone with your partner can improve your relationship. A study by the Marriage Foundation shows that couples that have a night out together just once a month are 14 per cent less likely to split up. It is easy to take each other for granted or even become frustrated with trivialities as you go through the motions of everyday life. Head out of the house and enjoy a walk together, or relive old times by doing something you used to enjoy, like seeing a band or going to a gallery. Laugh together and let yourselves go for a while. It doesn't have to involve red roses and champagne. It's the simple act of spending quality time together that makes the difference.

Divide your time

While it's lovely to spend time in a group, and it leads to laughter and fun and camaraderie, sometimes your loved ones benefit the most from having you all to themselves. Set aside time to do something with just one of your children or parents, instead of trying to find an activity that suits everyone together. There is nothing wrong with having a pedicure with your mum and then walking the dog separately with your dad. Cuddle up and watch cartoons with your youngest child, and then take your eldest child to spend their birthday money with your undivided attention. The greatest bonus of all is for you, who gets double the amount of hygge by splitting up your time!

Learn to listen

Conversation is, of course, a two-way interaction. Hygge is best created by caring, sharing, and listening. With only a plate of biscuits and a pot of tea in between you and a friend, life's obstacles can be tackled together. Be mindful that a good listener is willing to relinquish their share of the chat. Learn the art of truly listening, which is hearing what your friend says without focusing on what you're going to say in reply. Ask well-timed questions, but don't spend your listening time on devising those questions and lose focus on what is being said.

Modern life

Much has been said and written about the enormous number of hours spent on screens and with technology in this day and age. While it's true that we can all benefit from ignoring our phones sometimes, and limiting the use of social media, there are many ways to incorporate tablets and televisions into our hygge plans. Make the most of on demand movies for fun family time. Scroll through the options as a group but take turns to have the casting vote. You'll be amazed how much you enjoy a silly romcom or crazy cartoon when you're all laughing together, and older family members can revive classics that can become firmly entrenched in the children's top ten.

Open house

You can extend the invitation beyond family members. Spread the word that you'll be watching a major sporting event, with nibbles and drinks for the build up. See who turns up to watch the big game with you. It's much cheaper than seeing it live and emotions ride high when everyone becomes involved. Allow plenty of time for post-match analysis as that's all part of the fun. Even non-sports fans can become caught up in the atmosphere, and it is surprising how few neutrals will be left in the room when the action starts. Young and old alike can whoop and cheer if they choose a side to support.

The youth of today

Remember that hygge is about respecting others' views and habits to bob along harmoniously. That applies to all age groups, not only to adults. Times have changed and the Internet is an undeniable part of children's lives. They may seem to spend hours watching video clips and posting images of their favourite celebrities and what they're wearing, but by showing an interest you are allowing them the right to choose what they do with their spare time. Ask them to show you something funny, or an item that makes them think about the future, or an activity they would like to be involved in. Give credence to their views, and appreciate that this is now how they learn about the world. Allow them to be kids, too; it's only their equivalent of reading a joke book or a comic and no one has to spend all of their time in worthy pursuits. And don't rule out the occasional family selfie, either. They deserve a place in the album in just the same way that formal snaps and studio shots do, and mark a moment in time when you were all together.

Chapter 8
Follow that thought

Hygge isn't the only Scandinavian concept that's buzzing in the media right now, nor the only one that urges us to look at our life and see what's missing, or focus on the good times.

Lagom

A Swedish word, *lagom* means "just enough, the right amount" and it targets a healthy balance between work and free time, between our standard of living and our happiness. Whereas hygge is about capturing moments through your week, lagom is more of a constant way of living. It is somewhat akin to the Goldilocks search for things that are not too big or too hot, not too small or too cold, but just right. There is no need to go overboard in life; knowing when to stop is the way to be content and a good citizen of the world.

Never too much

The Swedish enjoy a high standard of living, but by keeping lagom in mind, they don't overindulge or live frivolously. A lot of consideration is given to saving water, reducing waste, and consuming in moderation, whether it be energy, food, or new clothes, and furniture. In some ways, it is taking a step back in time to the days when people didn't live on credit, or throw away food, or have six different choices of jacket for an evening out. For those with a tendency to overindulge, it may be the way forward. For others with an already balanced approach to life, it may seem like common sense.

Fika

Fika is another Swedish word, and is a coffee break done Scandi-style – that is, with the emphasis as much on the "break" as the "coffee". Forget grabbing a latte-to-go and drinking it on the move. Fika is a full stop in the middle of your morning, and your afternoon, when you down tools and take a break. There is food involved, too; usually cake or biscuits – giving us a hygge moment.

Take a break

Like hygge, fika is best done with a friend. Yet another word that translates into a sentiment rather than a single word, fika encapsulates the whole act of getting together with someone for coffee and a catch-up, with a tasty treat thrown in to keep you going and boost your spirits. Call round to see a friend, armed with a couple of pastries, homemade cakes, or even just a packet of cookies. Go to the desk of a colleague and invite her or him out into the sunshine. The difference between fika and a mere coffee break is that fika is not a guilty moment grabbed when the occasion allows, but a break that is rightfully yours and should be taken every day.

Scandi design

Strictly speaking, Scandinavia covers only three countries: Norway, Sweden and Denmark. Culturally, however, Finland and Iceland are often included, and several Icelandic and Finnish designers are lauded as part of the Scandinavian school. Their emphasis is on designs that improve everyday life, and that are functional and practical as well as visually appealing. Scandi design embraces durability and sustainability, and inspiration is taken from nature and organic forms, whether it be textures and patterns from trees, plants or ice, or the curved lines of lakes and rivers.

Day after day

Modern Scandinavian designs are built to last even with everyday use. They don't scream "look at me" with ornate embellishments or fanciful decoration. Instead, they are subtly attractive and often a joy to touch, hold, sit in or work with. Designers produce many different items for the home, from furniture to textiles and cutlery, ceramics and lighting, and many begin their training as architects. Their items are intended to be utile and not just put on show. Forget about "Sunday best" sets of curlicued silver cutlery and gold edged tableware that can't be washed in the dishwasher. Instead, knives and forks are forged from stainless steel, with simple forms that sit comfortably in your hand. Furniture is crafted with smooth lines and curves that beg you to sit down. No item is too insignificant to warrant careful design, from wine coolers to watering cans.

A sense of style

A Scandi home is likely to be decorated in a monochrome scheme with accents of colour or metallics: copper, brass and bronze are favourites. The general style is uncluttered, but that doesn't mean your home has to be starkly minimalist or coldly utilitarian. Many collectors combine stylish, sleek surroundings with a sense of humour shown through an occasional wacky artwork or lively collected pieces. Furniture that might add to the clutter is given a sleek appearance so it adds to the appeal of a room; audio equipment is a prime example of once-clunky items that have become stylish and sought-after additions to a home.

One for all

One of the overriding tenets of Scandinavian design is that beauty and quality should be available to everyone, not just rich collectors. It combines traditional craftsmanship and sustainable materials with the benefits of mass-production. That hands the notion of style back to the individual: how will you choose pieces and arrange and combine them in your own way, to prevent your house looking like a show home? The Scandinavian design school has made a name for itself since the 1930s, so there are plenty of classics. Look for chairs by Arne Jacobsen and Hans Wegner, ceramics by Lovisa Wattmann, candleholders by Mogens Lassen, and the block lamp by Harri Koskinen.

Mindfulness

Hygge goes hand in hand with another concept that is widely known these days: mindfulness. Like hygge, mindfulness is a way to step off the rollercoaster of modern living and take the time to appreciate more of what's happening around you. It helps you to notice the world at large, and to comprehend your feelings and thoughts in relation to it. Being more mindful allows us to understand ourselves better, enjoy life more and improve our mental wellbeing.

Mind supervision

It is easy to feel out of control when the pace of life is so fast. Mindfulness puts you back in charge of the things that are within you – your emotional responses and decisions. It allows you to observe what is happening inside, without judgement or criticism, and be kinder to yourself. We are encouraged to notice our negative feelings, thoughts, fears, and judgements as they arise, make a mental note of them, identify what they are, and then let them pass without getting bogged down about what they mean and how we will handle them. This stops the descent into a spiral of self-accusation and destructive behaviour such as comfort eating, insomnia, irritability, and addiction. It is important to acknowledge that notions come and go, and even negative ones will pass, so long as you let them. You don't have to act on all your thoughts but can file them or blow them on their way.

Looking with new eyes

Mindfulness is also a way to reawaken feelings and experiences that we have begun to take for granted. It is something that everyone can achieve, to differing degrees. For some people, simply taking better note of what their senses are telling them is enough: sniffing the scent of the first rain on hot ground, or feeling the change in the breeze on a walk with the dog. Other people want more, and practise meditation to get it. Learn how to pull your thoughts back as they wander, and be patient: meditation is a skill that has to be learnt, like any other. Tai chi and yoga can also help with meditation, as well as improving your body physically.

Reclaim your brain

Don't think that this approach is about seeing the world through rose-tinted glasses or putting your head in the sand and not seeing it at all. It is about seeing things with better perspective and a clearer vision, and being able to tackle them appropriately and wisely. Break away from long-formed habits, even if it is swapping seats on the train or at the meal table, or taking a different route home sometimes. Take your life back; flick off the autopilot setting and start living a varied and colourful life again.

"Whatever you are, be a good one"
— Abraham Lincoln

The Slow Movement

The Slow Movement began as a reaction to fast food but has spread to encompass so many things: travel, fashion, parenting, education, work and the media, to name just some. The message behind the Slow Movement is that a faster-paced life is not necessarily a better one. Similarly, getting what you want instantly does not lead to a greater appreciation of it; in fact, most would agree that it lessens the satisfaction. Just like hygge, the Slow Movement encourages us to consume less and enjoy things more.

The route to right

Zooming through life at top speed prevents us from really engaging with things. The more we rush, the less we savour the moment; the memories we make are more hazy and short-lived. The Slow Movement suggests that today's society has become so obsessed with where we're going that we don't enjoy the journey to get there, and we are missing out in so many ways. Life isn't just about ticking off things from our to-do list, but about achieving greatness in what we do, and taking pleasure from it. Things don't always have to be done slowly, but at the correct speed – that's how to get things right.

Making the connection

Sometimes our body regulates our speed of living for us; we push it to the limit and then get ill, which is a physical way of making us slow down or stop and recuperate. Even then, many people push on through, ignoring the warning signs and driving themselves to the ground. The Slow Movement emphasises the importance of connections: connecting to

what our body tells us about our well-being, and on a much larger scale, connecting to our family, our neighbours and community, and our land and the food it provides. Slow Food rejects mass-production that delivers homogenised food all around the world. It celebrates local goods, traditional recipes, seasonal produce, and the education of the younger generation about where food comes from before it is on the shelves.

Dress code

The Slow Movement encompasses hygge ideals through and through. It admonishes the instant waste of fast food packaging and cartons, but also the attitude of "if it isn't broken, don't fix it". Instead of throwing belongings away and buying new ones, we should be mending or tending them so they don't break in the first place, and borrowing instead of replacing items willy-nilly. Similarly, Slow Fashion encourages making and mending, and buying fewer items less often instead of overloading our lives with consumerism.

KonMari

Most of us don't even notice that we have gathered huge amounts of stuff until we have to locate something vital, or our children leave home, or we move house. The KonMari method, devised and outlined by Marie Kondo, is a way of tidying your home to declutter your living space, freeing up your mental ties to objects and possessions as you do so. It may not sound all that hygge, but the very essence of KonMarie is looking for things that make you happy and keeping them close by. Kondo's rule of thumb is to work through items and keep only the ones that "spark joy" – what could be more hygge than that?

Life without clutter

We often cling on to things for the wrong reasons, and this can weigh us down. That attic full of boxes that you never even look inside? It is literally a weight hanging over you. A desk full of papers, a bathroom full of products, a wardrobe full of clothes: they are all preventing you from moving quickly and efficiently through your home or your daily life, and they get in the way of using and relishing the things you really love.
It is important, though, that you don't look for things to throw out. Instead, look for the items you want to keep – those things that really bring you happiness.

Major project

The KonMari method instructs us to deal with one category of belongings at a time, beginning with clothes, then books, then papers, then miscellaneous items. There are so many of these, not all personal, and once you get started, you may not want to stop.

Tackle boxes of school artwork you have saved, souvenirs and programmes, tools in the shed, even your food cupboard, stores of craft items, bedding, towels, and toiletries and cosmetics. They may not all resonate with memories but it feels good to clear out tins and boxes or creams and lipsticks whose best before dates expired long ago.

Work methodically

Work on one category at a time rather than one room at a time, as similar items are often distributed throughout the house. Gather everything in one space, and then pick up each item to consider it close up instead of viewing things from a distance. The rule is: if you don't love it, don't keep it. Don't find a home for the items you intend to keep until the very end; discard anything unwanted before you place things back. Fold items and store them vertically. Aim to keep it that way, with a place for everything and everything in its place.

Index

activities 10, 74–83, 110
allotment 41, 94
autumn 84, 86, 93, 94

baking 8, 38, 41, 46
barbecues 49, 89
bees 84
blankets 20, 23
board games 42, 97

cake 10, 24, 33, 38, 39, 42, 46, 49, 51, 61, 69, 74, 82, 100, 118
cake stand, 33
camping 89
candles 10, 13, 16, 19, 23, 25, 33, 74, 93, 96, 97, 103, 120
children 8, 10, 14, 30, 38, 39, 41, 42, 48, 74, 78, 84, 89, 90, 99, 100, 103, 104, 110, 113, 114, 117, 126
Christmas 100–109
clothing 37, 74, 89, 96, 106, 118, 126
colours 20, 103, 106
comfort food 10, 51
cooking 8, 9, 14, 37, 41, 42, 45, 49, 89
crafts 32–35, 82, 99, 103, 104–109, 126
cycling 14, 74, 89

decorating 20, 23, 28, 103, 106, 120
Denmark 4, 6, 13, 14, 19, 37, 49, 51, 74, 94, 113, 120

eco-friendly 14, 106
exercise 14, 38, 114
family 4, 6, 8, 10, 12, 23, 25, 34, 38, 42, 74, 94, 97, 99, 100, 103, 104, 106, 110–117, 125
festivals 77, 99
Fika 118
Finland 4, 120
fire 10, 13, 16, 17, 19, 23, 37, 42, 77, 81, 86, 90, 96
flowers 20, 23, 27, 28, 84, 93, 94
food 4, 6, 10, 13, 14, 38–73, 77, 78, 82, 86, 94, 100, 118, 125, 126
foraging 94
friends 6, 8, 14, 16, 24, 27, 30, 32, 38, 39, 41, 42, 45, 46, 48, 74, 77, 78, 84, 89, 96, 99, 106, 110–117, 118, 120
furniture 20, 23, 24, 30, 42, 46, 48, 49, 77, 100, 103, 118, 120, 122
garden 8, 28, 30 49, 77, 82, 84, 86, 93, 94, 110, 113
gifts 10, 28, 30, 42, 94, 100, 106, 108

homes 8, 9, 10, 14, 16–37, 41, 42, 48, 77, 78, 94, 97, 99, 103, 104, 113, 120, 122, 126
hormones 14, 38

Iceland 4, 120

KonMarie 126

Lagom 118
lighting 13, 19, 20, 25, 37, 89, 90, 93, 99, 103

markets 41, 42, 78
mental health 14

mindfulness 122
nature 6, 20, 23, 27, 28, 30, 84, 86, 89, 94, 120
Norway 13, 120

parenting 110, 125
pets 8, 23, 27, 33, 38, 84, 86, 114, 122
photographs 23, 30, 99, 106
picnics 14, 48, 74, 93
plants 27, 28, 84, 90, 93, 94, 120
rain 4, 10, 16, 77, 81, 86, 122
recycling 27, 105
reusing 14, 27, 82

Scandinavia 4, 6, 14, 37, 74, 89, 118, 120
seasons 14, 41, 42, 82, 84–99, 125
shopping 78, 82
Slow Movement 125
snow 4, 8, 14, 74, 78, 81, 96, 99, 103, 105
social media 8, 78, 117
socks 13, 37, 74, 97
soft furnishings 20
spring 28, 84, 85, 86, 93
stress 8, 14, 37, 41, 46, 81, 99, 100
summer 4, 13, 19, 48, 49, 51, 77, 84, 89, 90, 93, 99

teenagers 13, 89
throws 10, 20, 24, 96

walking 8, 14, 30, 38, 41, 45, 48, 74, 77, 84, 86, 89, 93, 113, 114, 122
winter 4, 13, 14, 16, 19, 20, 37, 77, 84, 86, 93, 96, 97, 99, 109